Wood Pallet
PROJECTS

Wood Pallet

P R O J E C T S

Cool and Easy-to-Make Projects for the Home and Garden

CHRIS GLEASON

Entry Caddy, page 66.

FOX CHAPEL
PUBLISHING

ISBN 978-1-56523-544-1

Cover photography:
Left: Trevor Elliott of Magnetic Grain, *www.magneticgrain.com*.
Upper right: Author Chris Gleason.
Bottom right: David Grant of Crate & Pallet, *www.crateandpallet.blogspot.com*.

Special thanks to Dana Awtry of Good Earth Furniture (*www.goodearthfurniture.com*), Dustin and Whitney Barrington of The Rooster and the Hen (*www.theroosterandthehen.com*), Joanna Billigmeier of Waiting for Two (*www.craftynester.com*), Amanda Carver of Amanda Carver Designs (*www.amandacarverdesigns.com*), Laura Distin of The Ironstone Nest (*www.theironstonenest.com*), Kristi Dominguez of I Should Be Mopping the Floor (*www.ishouldbemoppingthefloor.com*), Trevor Elliott of Magnetic Grain (*www.magneticgrain.com*), Stacy K. Ercan and Danielle Wieland of Stacy K Floral (*www.stacykfloral.com*), David Grant of Crate & Pallet (*www.crateandpallet.blogspot.com*), Kat Hertzler of Maple Leaves & Sycamore Trees (*www.mapleleavessycamoretrees.com*), Rogier Jaarsma (*www.rogierjaarsma.nl*), Jonas Merian of Jonas' Design (*www.jonasdesign.net*), Mom and Her Drill (*www.momandherdrill.blogspot.com*), Emilie Perez of Crème Anglaise (*www.cremeanglaiseuk.canalblog.com*), Amber Puzey of Pineplace (*www.pineplace.com*), Sheryl Salisbury of Sheryl Salisbury Photography (*www.sherylsalisburyphotography.com*), Nathan and Katie Streu of If I Weren't So Lazy… (*www.ifiwerentsolazy.blogspot.com*), Kierste Wade of Brown Paper Packages (*www.brownpaper--packages.com*), Jenna Wilson of Wilsons & Pugs (*www.wilsonsandpugs.blogspot.com*), and Lori Danelle Wilson of Lori Danelle (*www.loridanelle.com*) for their kind contributions to the gallery.

The photos from Leonora Enking and various brennemans on pages 24 and 30 have been used under the Creative Commons Attribution-ShareAlike 2.0 Generic (CC BY-SA 2.0) license. The photo from eren (sea + prairie) on page 26 has been used under the Creative Commons Attribution 2.0 Generic (CC BY 2.0) license. The photo from ann-dabney on page 30 has been used under the Creative Commons Attribution-NoDerivs 2.0 Generic (CC BY-ND 2.0) license. To learn more, visit *www.creativecommons.org/lecrnses*.

Library of Congress Cataloging-in-Publication Data

Gleason, Chris, 1973-
 Wood pallet projects / Chris Gleason.
     pages cm
 Includes index.
 Summary: "Lumber prices are soaring, and deforestation is a rising concern. Yet millions of pounds of perfectly usable wood are dumped in landfills every year. Wood Pallet Projects shows how anyone can upcycle salvaged pallet wood to create truly one-of-a-kind projects. Maverick craftsman Chris Gleason combines sound woodworking techniques with a hip designer's sensibility to unleash the limitless possibilities of the common skid. Inside you'll find 15 of his inspired projects for rescuing and repurposing pallets. Some of his pieces celebrate the rough, edgy character of the material, while others are crafted as fine furniture. He shows how to construct both indoor and outdoor furniture in a variety of styles, along with other useful items such as a birdhouse, a toolbox, and even a ukulele. There's plenty of nitty gritty here on working with pallets, including where to find them, how to process them into usable lumber, fasteners, sanding, and the best finishes (if any) to use. The author provides important advice on how to make sure that your pallets are safe, and not sprayed with harmful chemicals. A colorful gallery of finished work provides further inspiration for green crafting"-- Provided by publisher.
 ISBN 978-1-56523-544-1 (pbk.)
 1. Woodwork--Patterns. 2. Pallets (Shipping, storage, etc.) 3. Salvage (Waste, etc.) I. Title.
 TT180.G545 2013
 684'.08--dc23
                    2012028942

To learn more about the other great books from Fox Chapel Publishing, or to find a retailer near you,
call toll-free 800-457-9112 or visit us at *www.FoxChapelPublishing.com*.

Note to Authors: We are always looking for talented authors to write new books. Please send a brief letter
describing your idea to Acquisition Editor, 1970 Broad Street, East Petersburg, PA 17520.

Printed in China
Fifth printing

ABOUT THE AUTHOR

Chris Gleason is the author of several books for the DIY market, including *Building Projects for Backyard Farmers and Home Gardeners*, *Art of the Chicken Coop*, *Built-In Furniture for the Home*, *The Complete Kitchen Makeover*, *Complete Custom Closet*, *Old-School Workshop Accessories*, and *Building Real Furniture for Everyday Life*. Gleason grew up on a farm in upstate New York and has been raising chickens in his Salt Lake City backyard for more than six years. He currently builds and sells chicken coops. He has owned Gleason Woodworking Studios for more than thirteen years.

CONTENTS

TRANSFORMED
From Skid Row to Sturdy & Stylish

Start with a pallet. Add some time and carpentry techniques. Finish with these!

Easy Home Accessories

Tea Light Holders: A Group of Rugged Optimists. Page 46.

Basic Box: Have It, Hold It, Keep It Real. Page 55.

Magazine Display Box: Show Your Rustic Stuff. Page 60.

Mirror or Picture Frame: Glimpse of Past and Future Glory. Page 49.

Furniture, Indoors and Out

Entry Caddy: Friendly and Reliable. Page 66.

Chair: Simple Meets Sophisticated. Page 71.

Outdoor Loveseat: Life of the Lawn Party. Page 85.

Coffee Table: Robust and Refined. Page 77.

Fun & Functional Projects

Birdhouse: A Homey and Hospitable Haven. Page 92.

Toolbox: Cool, Collected, Capable. Page 97.

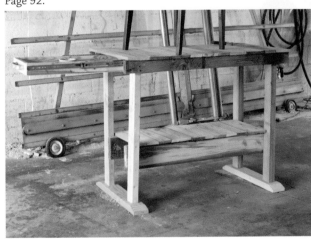

Workbench: Doing a Job Well. Page 103.

Ukulele: Music in the Key of 'Pallet'. Page 109.

ABOUT WOOD PALLET PROJECTS

Wood pallets have long been vital to shipping processes. Much more recently, they have become popular for home and outdoor projects. It's not hard to see why. Pallet wood is cheap (often free for the taking), and using it is a form of recycling.

Perhaps more important than that, though, is its character. All wood is unique, with its own organic characteristics, but pallets add to that a patina, if you will, of experience. They are weathered; they are distressed; they are aged. They have served a purpose, and are ready for more. They are beautiful in a way that shiny new things can never be.

My goal in this book is to show just how versatile pallet wood can be, and to demonstrate how thoughtful craftspeople can use it to build functional objects in a broad range of styles. I enjoy showcasing both the sleek and the rough, on various levels, and I found creating these projects very satisfying.

Start with "Breaking It Down," which offers guidelines for selecting and salvaging pallets. Browse "Palletpalooza," a gathering of innovative pallet constructions from all over, for inspiration. Then, move on to the projects section, which offers step-by-step instructions for constructing everything from a simple tea light holder to an outdoor loveseat to a ukulele. Create one or more of those twelve projects for your home, yard, or shop, or simply read through the instructions as primers for how to effectively work with pallet wood.

Finally, check out the interesting and informative tidbits scattered throughout the pages. I guarantee you'll learn something!

 Fact An inch of wood is fifteen times more efficient as an insulator than an inch of concrete.

 Coffee Table, page 77.

BREAKING IT DOWN
How to be an Effective Scavenger

Pallets offer a great opportunity to obtain free materials for little or (usually) no money, and this fact alone makes them worth considering as a resource. However, not all pallets are created equal or are suitable for your project. Here are my tricks of the pallet-scavenging trade.

Permission: Always Get It

It's the golden rule of scavenging pallets: **Always ask permission first.**
Many businesses that use pallets actually recycle them. They may use the pallets repeatedly, or the supplier might pick up the pallets and reimburse them for returning them.

So before you help yourself to what you think may be free, remember that if you don't have permission it could also be viewed as theft. Just ask. Some businesses will be delighted to have you take extra pallets off their hands.

▶▶▶ BEWARE BACTERIA
Even if a pallet was clean and dry and safe on the day it was manufactured, it could have been exposed to undesirable bacteria sometime during its lifetime. To play it safe, scrub the wood with bleach and soapy water. Rinse well, and allow to completely dry. Remember, wood is porous, so there's a chance the bacteria is embedded. Don't use pallet wood for food-related items, children's toys, or children's play furniture. It just isn't worth the risk.

This stack might contain some great projects.

 Many companies are going green by reusing their own pallets.

Safety: Know Which Pallets to Use and Which to Avoid

Most pallets are perfectly fine to work with, but some aren't. Chances are that the pallet you're working with is safe, but what if it was treated with some kind of chemical earlier in its life? I've also been emailed with a story in which someone got a nasty sliver from a pallet that introduced infection, requiring hospitalization.

So, just be picky. Always wear gloves and choose wisely. When in doubt, leave it out. But how can you tell?

Fortunately, it is straightforward. My goal is to provide facts, not cause unnecessary concern. Common sense is your best starting point. Skip any that:

- Are unusually heavy
- Are wet
- Appear greasy
- Have stains
- Smell
- Display too many twisted nails
- Otherwise look unsavory

Beyond that, what else can you look for? Many pallets are stamped "HT" for heat-treated, which is a good sign that the pallet is newer and was kiln-dried to remove moisture, which could otherwise turn into a problem. Remember, if a pallet isn't dry, it'll be a pain to work with, and it could harbor bacteria, so give it a pass.

Some pallets are even stamped with a 1-800 phone number or website that lets you know about the pallet's origins. You probably don't need to get on the phone or fire up a web browser: the mere presence of an indicator like this is a very good sign that the pallet was produced as carefully as possible. These pallets are probably good candidates for your projects, provided they meet your other basic criteria (i.e., clean, dry, good condition, etc.).

Label	Meaning
HT	Heat-treated
KD	Kiln Dried
MB	Methyl bromide treated
DB	Debarked
S-P-F	Contains spruce, pine, or fir components

The stamp indicates that this pallet was kiln dried (a.k.a. heat-treated) and is made of spruce, pine, or fir components (S-P-F). This pallet went onto my "keeper" pile.

Pedigree stamps are a good sign, often indicating that a responsible company has produced the pallet to be as safe as possible. If you want more detailed information, call or check the website on the stamp, in this case *www.palletid.info*. International Plant Protection Convention (IPPC) stamps indicate the pallet has been treated to prevent the transportation of pests between countries. IPPC stamps list the country of origin, the facility number, and the method of treatment.

Suitability: Is It A Good Match For Your Project?

The key to working with pallets is strategy. Having a project in mind will guide your assessment. The first question is, does this pallet merit a second glance or should I move on? If it looks promising, you'll want to ascertain the following.

- Is it safe?
- Are there any especially appealing boards (due to species, interesting character, or useful dimensions)?
- How much usable material does it contain?
- How easy will it be to disassemble? For example, softwood runners are easier to get nails out of than hardwood ones. With a little practice, you'll be able to see the difference at a glance.

The answers to these questions, in aggregate, will determine which pallets are worth your time and effort. Sometimes I will only take one board from a pallet, as I don't have infinite time and energy to spend on tasks that only offer a marginal yield. Is this the optimal level of upcycling? Maybe not, but I don't try to take on the responsibility of reusing every piece of material in all of the world's pallets; once you view the situation through this lens, it is easy to see that even partial reuse is certainly better than none at all. In other cases, I *can* use the whole thing.

When it comes to pallet disassembly, a methodical approach pays off. Take a minute to decide which parts of the pallet are the most important to you. You may not have a premium use for all of the wood, due to damaged pieces, odd sizes, or the presence of way too many nails in a given spot.

Pallet sizing

Wood pallets come in all shapes and sizes, and depending on where you live, you will encounter pallets of many different dimensions. In North America, for example, some common pallet sizes include 48" x 48" (about 1200 x 1200mm), 48" x 20" (about 1200 x 500mm), and 36" x 36" (about 900 x 900mm). In Europe, common sizes include 1200 x 1000mm (about 48" x 40"), 800 x 1200mm (about 30" x 48"), and 600 x 400mm (about 20" x 15"). The great thing about pallets, however, is it doesn't matter what shape or size they come in, as long as you can harvest wood of the dimensions you need from them. Only one project in this book requires the use of a full, intact pallet (see page 85). All the others can be made from wood harvested from pallets and cut to size.

Dealing with nails

Pallets are usually built with nails, because it is a low-tech but strong approach. If you take a close look, you'll see that many of the nails are spiral-shaped; this is because their unique shape helps them resist backing out and allowing the boards to loosen over time. Spiral nails are good for constructing pallets, but can create a challenge for someone who is actually trying to remove the nails to get at usable lumber. My standard approach is to pull the nails using a crowbar or similar tool if it isn't too time-consuming, and to leave them in when removal isn't feasible. This latter approach usually means cutting around the nail-infested areas and harvesting shorter, but still useful, lengths.

Occasionally, I'll have nails that refuse to budge from a piece of wood that I still really want to use: in cases like this, I cut the nails back as far as possible using a hand-held rotary grinder, angle grinder, or pliers. I then use a belt sander to ensure the nail heads are flush to the surface. This approach is neat because the polished nail heads gleam nicely and recall the wood's origins as a humble pallet.

Learn to recognize the inherent limits of some pallets. Occasionally, I'll come across a pallet that features really pretty wood, but the nails are just torture to remove. In this case, cutting out the largest nail-free

Manufacturers like spiral-cut nails; pallet scavengers—not so much.

A rotary tool equipped with a metal-cutting disc is a fast, easy way to cut nails flush.

sections of wood possible is the best decision. It may mean settling for shorter lengths of wood than you'd ideally like, but it will allow you to work safely with the material. If you need larger pieces, find a pallet that will allow you to harvest them more easily, and save the short pieces for another day. You'll eventually find a project that they're better suited for. It is also worth noting that changing your design and/or construction techniques might allow you to use the shorter pieces right away, too.

Getting good lumber from pallets is easy if you know how, and this basic tool kit makes it a snap to "harvest" useful boards.

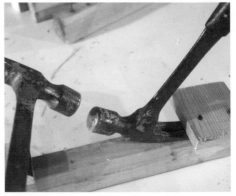

My pallet-disassembly toolkit includes two hammers because I've often found this little trick more effective than using a crowbar.

Sometimes the nails themselves aren't the only problem: boards are sometimes prone to splitting in the areas where nails have been inserted, especially if the nails are close to the end of the board. In this case, I usually just cut off the cracked portion so I have a clean end to start with. If cutting off the end isn't an option—i.e., you really need the extra length for a given project—you might be able to force glue into the crack and clamp it shut. While this method isn't guaranteed to work, it can be worth a try, and it doesn't take very long, so you're not out a lot of time and energy if the crack reopens.

The good thing about nails in pallets is that they are placed fairly predictably: you won't generally find random nails occurring in random places. Manufacturers have no incentive to place nails at irregular intervals. So, if you got all of the nails out of the obvious places, you can generally feel fine about sending a board through a planer, jointer, or table saw.

Don't be afraid to move things around when you're working with pallets: use the floor, a workbench, or whatever else works. Finer tasks like pulling nails are often most easily accomplished on a bench, whereas larger-scale tasks like tearing apart pallets will probably occur with the pallet on the ground. Jump right in, and you'll get a feel for it in about five minutes.

DON'T RUN BOARDS WITH NAILS THROUGH MACHINERY

Under no circumstances should a board with even one nail in it be run through a planer or across a table saw or jointer. This is not only ruinous for the blades, but a nail that makes contact with a blade can be propelled back toward the operator at shocking speeds. Don't let it happen—even by accident.

Incorporating 'defects'

Sometimes surface characteristics such as nail holes, stains, and the rough texture that results from the minimal amount of milling that the wood received can be kind of appealing.

Designing with the limitations of the materials in mind may help. Trying to build very refined items with rough-sawn wood takes some skill, but it can be done. One approach is to embrace the character of the wood rather than fight it. If you're working with rough, uneven boards, allowing your designs to have an organic rather than a regimented feel might be rather liberating. Many designers who work with pallets like to show off the origins of the material rather than hide it. The chair that I build for this book shows a design that I think balances crisp modern lines and weathered, organic textures.

All materials have limitations, and many designers have said that design is the process of working with limitations to get the best result at the most reasonable cost. Working with pallets is a wonderful way of embracing wood in a very "organic" state—they're all different.

Cracks like those on the ends of this board are a common defect in pallet wood. In this case, they don't extend more than a few inches, so I chose to simply cut off the cracked portion. The remaining slat was still long enough to be useful.

Sycamore is one of my favorite woods, and it is prized for the unusual flecks in its grain pattern. It is almost hard to believe that these two boards came from a discarded pallet!

 Fact   **Pallet materials that have been heat-treated must be marked HT.**

Tools: The Basics

It is fitting that a material as humble as pallet wood can be successfully worked with even the most basic woodworking tools. The simplest projects may require nothing more than hand tools—a sharp handsaw can cut through pallet wood surprisingly quickly, and a good old-fashioned hammer and nails might be all you need to make sturdy joints. If you're just getting started in woodworking, this might be a good place to start. Over time, you can always get more tools—the classified ads might be a good place to find some bargains—*and* the expertise to use them safely. To get you started, this section will provide a quick overview of some basic and not-so-basic tools that might come in handy when working with pallet wood.

Hand tools

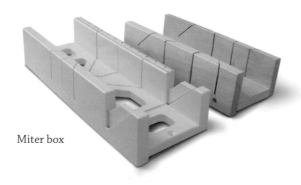

Miter box

You want to use these workshop basics for cutting your pallet wood.

Carpenter's saw. This is your basic handsaw, which can be used for cutting pallet boards to size. Keep this saw sharp and you'll have no trouble cutting through pallet wood.

Miter box. Use this with your carpenter's saw to cut accurate angles for joints, such as box corners.

Coping saw. This saw is made for cutting curves and making other non-linear cuts. You can use this saw to shape your pallet boards into something more unique and visually interesting.

Dozuki backsaw. This saw is perfect for cutting wood pieces flush to a surface, as the teeth have no set. In other words, they don't flare out to the sides beyond the blade.

Coping saw

Fact   Heat sterilization is the most practical way to keep pallets from transporting insects.

Handheld power sanders

Use these sanders to turn the rough, worn exterior of your pallet wood into a smooth, sophisticated surface.

Belt sanders. Many belt sanders have a lock that secures the trigger in the "on" position. Consequently, make sure your sander is turned off before plugging it into your power source. Failure to check the trigger could result in a runaway tool that can easily cause damage and injury. One horror story I've heard tells of a man who put his belt sander on a nearly completed tabletop—needless to say, irreparable scarring resulted. On the flip side, a small, but mighty, belt sander racing league exists to celebrate the unique locomotive quality of this tool under controlled conditions.

Random orbit sander. This tool allows you to quickly sand pallet boards, but it does have a tendency to leave swirls in the wood that must be sanded away with fine-grit sandpaper.

Finishing sander. Use 180-grit sandpaper, or higher, with this sander for a great final sanding. The even sanding this tool provides helps prepare a surface for finishes like stains, varnishes, or paints.

While a runaway belt sander in your workshop is a major problem, under controlled conditions, a belt sander race can be an exciting event for both participants and spectators.

Random orbit and pad sanders

 SANDPAPER SUCCESS

To achieve maximum smoothness for your projects, you need to change the sandpaper in your power sanders frequently. As soon as you notice it is taking longer than usual for your sander to produce the effect you want, swap out the paper. If you're worried these frequent changes will waste sandpaper, hang on to old pieces and save them for a time when you need fine-grit paper. A piece of worn 100-grit sandpaper can easily take the place of a fresh 180-grit piece.

Handheld power saws

For those projects where your trusty carpenter's saw just won't cut it, these are some of the power saws you can use to get the job done.

Circular saw. This is my go-to saw for making handheld straight cuts in a variety of materials.

Jigsaw. If I could buy only one saw, it would be a quality jigsaw. This saw is able to cut curves with great precision and will also cut thick stock. When purchasing a jigsaw, it's good to note that not all are created equal; newer models tend to be more powerful and precise than their predecessors.

Reciprocating saw. This saw is particularly useful for tearing apart pallets. With the right blade installed, you can also use it to cut through nails.

Circular saw

Jigsaw

Fact   Heat-treated pallets are weaker than non-treated ones.

Large Woodworking Machines

Machines like these can speed things up tremendously, and they may even take your pallet projects to a whole new level. Even if you don't have the time, space, or desire for a full-blown woodworking shop filled with these types of machines, you might be able to find a woodworking shop in your area where you can do some work. Continuing education classes might be a good resource to tap into if you're stumped on where to begin.

Thickness planer. This machine features a row of sharp knives that spins on a round cutterhead. By adjusting the height of the infeed table, you can plane boards to nearly any thickness you might require.

Jointer. Use this machine to create a smooth edge or face on a board. When two boards have been "jointed" on their edges, they can be glued together with a barely noticeable seam.

Table saw. Most woodworking shops are organized around a table saw, because it is such an important and versatile tool. If your space or funds are limited, a simple table saw can be purchased new for less than $150, and it can easily be set up outdoors if that helps you save space.

Drill press. While it isn't necessary for most projects, a drill press is a handy addition to most shops. Once you're used to having one on hand, you'll wonder how you ever got by without it.

Band saw. Band saws are wonderful tools, because they allow you to quickly make non-linear cuts in both wood and metal. Curved shapes can be cut freehand, which makes the band saw a nice complement to the table saw, which excels at cutting straight lines.

Adjustable miter saw. This is a great tool for cutting stock to length. You can also adjust the angle of the cut.

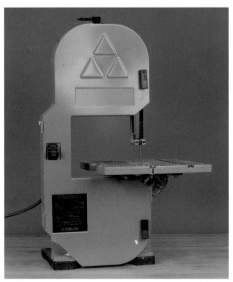

Drill press

PALLETPALOOZA
A Planet of Possibilities

The world of repurposed pallets is wonderfully creative. Here are some ideas to jump-start your brainstorming.

Photo courtesy of Jonas Merian of Jonas' Design, *www.jonasdesign.net*.

LOW SEATS

These low seats look perfectly suited to their environment: a large, open-plan loft like this might need casual seating for parties and gathering, and this design allows for seating that can be spontaneously moved around with ease. The upholstered tops make them quite inviting, and I imagine that one could push a pair of them together to create a guest bed.

Photos courtesy of Jonas Merian of Jonas' Design, *www.jonasdesign.net*.

ROLLING BENCHES

The rolling benches in this room are a favorite for me,
I must admit. The long, skinny proportions are interesting,
and I am especially attracted to the finish on the top. The
boards have just the right weathered look to them, and they
contrast so perfectly with the lumber on the base.

Photos courtesy of Rogier Jaarsma, www.rogierjaarsma.nl.

GREEN OFFICE SPACE

The BrandBase office in Amsterdam, Netherlands, used pallets to create a completely unique workspace. Throughout the office, pallets form desks, tables, and even staircases.

Photos courtesy of Rogier Jaarsma, *www.rogierjaarsma.nl*.

STORE DISPLAYS

What better way to display items for sale at a nursery than on top of tables and display stands that are built from the pallets that the items were shipped on? Talk about a circle of life!

Photos courtesy of Leonora Enking.

This approach is quite handy because it allows the displays to be built in whatever shapes are more useful.

Fact If you're into recycling, you'll love pallets; they're made from a renewable resource and are reusable, repairable, and recyclable!

Photos courtesy of Trevor Elliott of Magnetic Grain, *www.magneticgrain.com*.

OUTDOOR LOUNGE SET

This outdoor lounge set is just beautiful. The fact that it consists of three matching pieces makes such a great visual impact: I think it shows how carefully tempered pallet wood can be used in a modern, refined décor.

EASILY MOVEABLE TABLE

It doesn't get much simpler than this, but the result is still utterly charming. Bolt a set of large casters (they look to be about 4" [102mm] in diameter to me) to the bottom of a pallet, and you've got an instant, low-to-the-ground, easily movable table. The rough, weathered quality of the wood on this pallet makes it ideally suited for outdoor use. It could be a perfect way to transport garden or yard tools around the backyard as you do some mulching or pruning.

Photo courtesy of eren {sea+prairie}.

Photo courtesy of Mom and Her Drill, *www.momandherdrill.blogspot.com*.

ACCENT WALL

An enterprising Mom took some pallets home from work and used them to create an accent wall in her living room. It took about twenty-five pallets to cover the wall. She used construction adhesive and a nail gun to attach the pallets, and then anchored the TV to a stud. The pallet wood is completely unfinished, without stain or polyurethane.

Photo courtesy of David Grant of Crate & Pallet, *www.crateandpallet.blogspot.com.*

TRUNK

I would welcome a nice piece of furniture like this into my own home. The zippy paint color and the pallet-wood pedigree offer just the right combo, in my opinion, of funky and finery. I love the unfinished interior of the trunk; it provides a lovely visual contrast with the bold primary paint color.

Photos courtesy of David Grant of Crate & Pallet, www.crateandpallet.blogspot.com.

Photo courtesy of David Grant of Crate & Pallet, www.crateandpallet.blogspot.com.

This trunk is sized just right so that it can do double duty as a coffee table. Nice! I love the way the maker used pallet wood but didn't skimp on quality joinery. On the front leg, for example, you can see the way the slats for the front and back of the trunk were placed into large grooves.

SERVING TRAY

This variation on a serving tray is beautiful. I can imagine using it to ferry things back and forth from the kitchen to the backyard during a barbecue. The distressed look of the paint adds a nice touch.

Photo courtesy of Dustin and Whitney Barrington of The Rooster and the Hen, *www.TheRoosterAndTheHen.com.*

HEADBOARD AND MIRROR FRAME

Pallet wood was used as an inexpensive way to transform this master bedroom. The boards for the headboard were whitewashed and sanded prior to disassembly. With the help of a stud finder and finishing nailer, the boards were then attached directly to the wall for an incredible floor-to-ceiling look. The mirror frame was built by gluing and nailing pallet boards into place around the frame of an old dresser mirror.

 Pallets are among the top recycled items in the United States.

Photo courtesy of Dustin and Whitney Barrington of The Rooster and the Hen, *www.TheRoosterAndTheHen.com.*

Photo courtesy of various brennemans.

PLANTER

Why not use a pallet as a planter? Somebody obviously took the time and effort to plant these pansies between the slats, but when I saw the blossoms for the first time, it looked like a spontaneous eruption of joy. I still like this photo as a neat reminder that good things can be planted in places you might not expect.

SIGNAGE

This is a great use for an old pallet. Talk about the medium being the message!

Photo courtesy of ann-dabney.

Photos courtesy of Stacy K. Ercan of Stacy K Floral, Rochester, New York, *www.stacykfloral.com*.
Photography by Danielle Wieland.

COLORFUL MOUNTED PLANTERS

These vertical gardens help save on space and are a perfect way to "up-cycle" average, everyday items into extraordinary creations! These unique wall gardens were made of materials that might be found at most businesses: wood pallets, spray paint, and burlap cloth.

Photo courtesy of Kristi Dominguez of I Should be Mopping the Floor, www.ishouldbemoppingthefloor.com, a website worth neglecting your shores for.

WALL ART

This pallet wall art piece was used to spruce up a master bedroom at almost no cost. The pallet was painted white with a gold heart, and then sanded and stained. Afterword, the stain was removed as well, creating a perfect, antiqued look.

Photo courtesy of Jenna Wilson of Wilsons & Pugs, *wilsonsandpugs.blogspot.com.*

WINE RACK

Pallet wood was put to good use to create this wine rack. The dark finish gives the piece an air of sophistication, and the design could easily be modified to display any number of items.

Photo courtesy of Nathan and Katie Streu of If I Weren't So Lazy…, *www.ifiwerentsolazy.blogspot.com.*

ROOM DIVIDER

A wall of pallets gives some separation to this big, open loft space. The pallets were purchased from a local warehouse for a dollar a piece and serve as the perfect location to hang photos, wall art, air plants, and other colorful items. Thin sheets of plywood and wallpaper can be added to the pallets for a unique design touch, or they can be left open as shown.

SHELF

The patina of the pallet makes this shelf, giving it the perfect weathered look. It was screwed directly into a wall using wall anchors.

Photo courtesy of Amanda Carver Designs, www.amandacarverdesigns.com. Photography by Amanda Carver.

RAISED GARDEN BEDS

Made of pallet wood and chicken wire, these raised garden beds
are perfect for growing all kinds of delicious fruits and veggies
while keeping pesky critters out.

 Fact   More than 150 million pallets are repaired for reuse or recycled each year.

OUTDOOR LOVESEAT

This outdoor loveseat is the perfect mix of fun and fashionable, with a funky back pattern and cushions and pillows in refined colors.

PORCH SWING

A simple pallet design adds charm to this porch. You could also suspend the swing from a tree, or even an indoor ceiling.

Photo courtesy of Kat Hertzler of Maple Leaves & Sycamore Trees, www.mapleleavessycamoretrees.com.

ACCENT CEILING

The varying shades of dark and light pallet wood used to create this accent ceiling add a unique twist to the design.

Photo courtesy of Amber Puzey of Pineplace, www.pineplace.com.

FARM TABLE

Pallet wood makes a sturdy, rustic table for family gatherings.

Photos courtesy of Emilie Perez of Crème Anglaise, www.cremeanglaiseuk.canalblog.com

PALLET CRIB

A husband and wife paired up to give pallet wood new life in the form
of this dreamy, whimsical moon baby bed. Take extra precautions when
selecting pallet wood for children's furniture. You want to make sure it
is sanitary and safe, so choose wisely, and scrub it well before use.

PERSONALIZED HEADBOARD

Personalized with a name and car design, this pallet headboard makes a great statement piece. The design is easy to customize by changing the name or symbol added to the headboard.

Photo courtesy of Amber Puzey of Pineplace, *www.pineplace.com.*

CHILD'S BED

What a creative use of pallet wood! Not only is this child's bed an extraordinary piece, the wheels on the bottom are practical, making it easy to move.

Photo courtesy of Lori Danelle Wilson of Lori Danelle, *www.loridanelle.com.*

Photo courtesy of Kierste Wade of Brown Paper Packages, *www.brownpaper--packages.com.*

BED FRAME

The design of this bed frame is so refined, it's hard to believe it started as pallet wood!

Photo courtesy of Joanna Billigmeier of Waiting for Two, *www.craftynester.com.*

COFFEE TABLES

Paint and stack a few pallets and you have a new coffee table for your family room. Use a paint or finish that will match the décor and style of your home. If you redecorate, simply sand the pallet down and start again.

 Fact For every ton of wood in a forest of young, growing trees, a ton of oxygen is produced and just as much carbon dioxide is absorbed.

Photos courtesy of Joanna Billigmeier of Waiting for Two, *www.craftynester.com.*

EASY HOME
Accessories

Working with pallets is all about transformation, right? You will take an aged, worn pallet and turn it into a new functional or decorative item while maintaining the unique character that makes pallet wood so special. While you're in the process of transforming your pallets, why not transform your home as well? Pallet wood is ideal for making items that can be incorporated into your everyday life.

The examples in this chapter include tea light holders, to add some ambience; a mirror or picture frame, for a unique feature piece; a basic box, for storage of all your most important items; and a magazine display box, to hold your favorite monthly publications. This is not where your pallet/home transformation has to end, though. Pallet pieces are perfect for any room in your home. Perhaps you can make a pallet tray for your kitchen, or use some small scrap pieces to put together a coaster holder. Before you buy it, try to build it—with a pallet!

Mirror or Picture Frame, page 49.

Tea Light Holders

A Group of Rugged Optimists

Even when my family sits down for a regular old weeknight dinner, we light a few candles. It is a small tradition we enjoy keeping, as it reminds us that even the simple things in life can be approached with an attitude of celebration. The essence of our system, if you can call it that, is to make our own tea light holders from scrap wood and then fill them with tea light candles that we buy in bulk. Because the candles are inexpensive, we can use them whenever we want. It is nice to have some in the backyard for alfresco dinners in the summer, for example, and in our dining room where we eat when the weather forces us indoors. It is also nice to have some extra tea light holders on hand to give away as gifts when the need arises. The best part about these tea light holders is you only need a few pieces of wood and a drill to make them.

One quick word of caution: I usually use a 1½" (38mm) drill bit to create the holes for the candles in my tea light holders. This has generally worked well with the tea lights we usually buy, but there was a time when we bought a pack of candles that didn't fit neatly into the 1½" (38mm) holes. It only happened once, but just be aware that tea light sizes may not be quite as uniform as one might assume!

Tea light holders can really be anything you choose to make them, so my instructions for this project are brief and include a number of examples of the different ways you can alter the designs of your tea light holders.

The basic steps

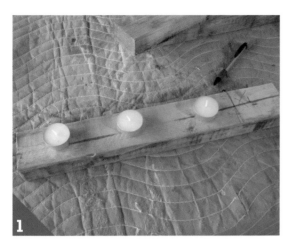

1 **Determine the position of the holes.** When I build a tea light holder that will incorporate multiple candles, I determine the placement of the holes for the candles by placing them on the wood piece and marking their positions.

2 **Drill the holes.** Drill a hole for each candle. I've found that a drill press does the best job of boring holes that are perpendicular to the top of the wood surface. While a drill press isn't essential, it is helpful if you have one at your disposal.

3 **Cut individual holders.** If you want to make individual tea light holders, cut your board into squares or rectangles, making sure you have a drilled hole in each piece.

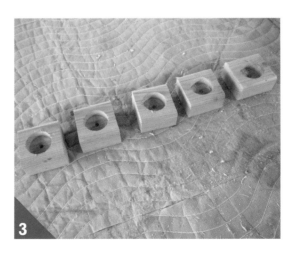

Fact Old pallets can be ground up to make insulation, landscaping mulch, and construction materials.

Adding embellishments

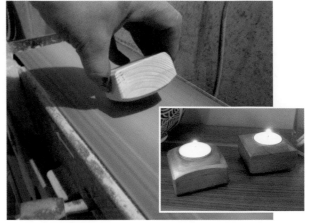

You can embellish your tea light holders with paint, a stain, pyrography, decorative edging, and more. In this case, I decided to rough up the sides of my tea light holder by cutting a series of saw kerfs on the table saw. Then, I stained it black and sanded away portions of the stain for a distressed look.

Use a stationary belt sander to soften the edges of your tea light holder or create facets. The silver spray paint I used on these holders does a fairly convincing job of creating the illusion that the holders are metal. Sanding off some of the paint and revealing the wood grain beneath then playfully subverts this illusion.

Individual tea lights can be reassembled in various ways, such as attached to another board or object (left) or stacked on top of one another to form a new shape (right).

Mirror or Picture Frame

Glimpse of Past and Future Glory

Making your own mirror or picture frames can save you a lot of money; the 13" x 13" (330 x 330mm) mirror I used for the project was cut from a scrap piece at my local home center, and it cost just $2. Factor in the free pallet materials and light labor, and I ended up with a one-of-a-kind piece for an unbeatable price. As you've probably realized, because the process for making picture frames is the same for making mirror frames, the instructions that follow can easily be used to make both. Professional picture framing is usually pretty expensive, so this is another great way to save money on home décor or gift items. Everybody likes a handmade frame.

There are many ways to make picture frames, and this section won't even try to detail them all—that could easily fill a whole book on its own! What I will do is detail the construction of a couple of types of frames and present some good starting points for making them yourself.

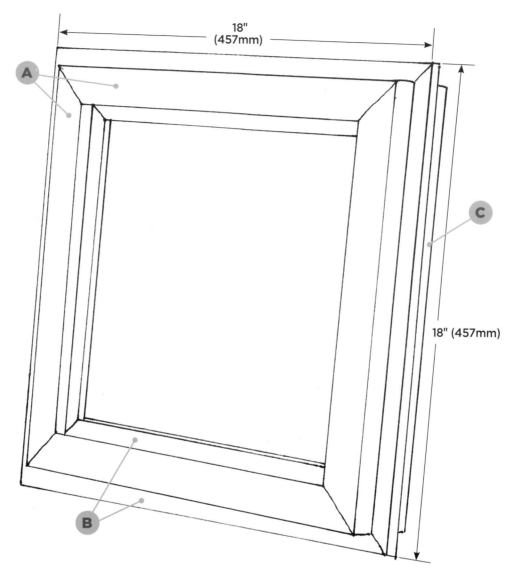

Mirror Frame Materials List*

	item	quantity	materials	dimensions
A	Top layer	4	¾" (19mm)-thick stock	1¼" x 18" (32 x 457mm)
B	Middle layer	4	¾" (19mm)-thick stock	2¼" x 18" (57 x 457mm)
C	Bottom layer	4	¾" (19mm)-thick stock	1" x 18" (25 x 457mm)

*Overall project dimensions are approximate

Fact Wood products are far more cost effective to produce than products made of other materials.

1 Select the wood. The process begins by harvesting a whole bunch of pallet wood. You'll want to make sure you have enough—it never hurts to err on the side of having extra—and that the pieces are all long enough to be of use.

2 Cut the materials to size. My next step was to rip the wood into the three different widths specified on the materials list (1", 1¼", and 2¼" [25mm, 32mm, and 57mm]). Then, I sent the wood through my planer to be skip-planed. Skip-planing will result in boards that do not have an entirely uniform thickness or surface. The process should get all of the frame pieces close enough to the proper size to work with—any discrepancies in thickness can quickly be removed by sanding. My boards for this project were about ¾" (19mm) thick.

3 Understand the layering. I ripped the stock into three different widths, essentially creating a layered molding that had a distinct groove up the middle and overhang on one edge. In this case, the groove is purely decorative, but the overhang serves to cover and secure the edge of the mirror. This built-up molding technique is pretty low-tech and user-friendly, which is why I like it. Other methods require a router to cut away a recess, which can be dangerous if you're not fully trained. This approach keeps it safe and simple.

4 Choose the molding style. After playing with a few different molding profiles, I settled on this one.

5 **Assemble the frame sides.** The strips were assembled as a stack with glue in between the layers and nails to hold them together while the glue dried. For each stack, I glued a 1" (25mm)-wide piece (C) to the bottom of a 2¼" (57mm)-wide piece (B), and a 1¼" (32)-wide piece (A) to the top.

6 **Miter one end.** A power miter box, or chop saw, is the fastest way to precisely cut miters on the ends of your frame boards, although you can also use a handsaw and miter box. Cut miters at one end of all four boards.

SIZING YOUR FRAME

For me, this mirror project was pretty casual: I worked with the materials I had on hand and let them dictate the size of the finished piece. You, however, may have some particular dimensions in mind for your frame. To make your frame a specific size, the recess at the back of the frame will be your starting point. In this case, let's imagine you're framing an 11" x 14" (279 x 356mm) item, and you're making a molding that will be 2" (51mm) wide. This means you'll need stock measuring at least 16" x 19" (406 x 483mm). How did I get these numbers? Multiply the width of the molding (2" or 51mm) by two, and add it to the dimensions of the object you're framing. Remember, the frame will have molding on all sides, so you'll want to add the width of the molding twice. Then, add an inch (25mm) to give you some wiggle room. So 11+2+2+1=16, and 14+2+2+1=19. After you cut a miter on one end of each frame board, you can then measure out 11" (279mm) along the inside of the rabbet on two boards, and 14" (356mm) on the remaining two. I suggest adding ¼" (6mm) to your desired final measurements to accommodate for any discrepancies in either the frame or the object being framed. You can then cut the miters on the opposing ends of the boards.

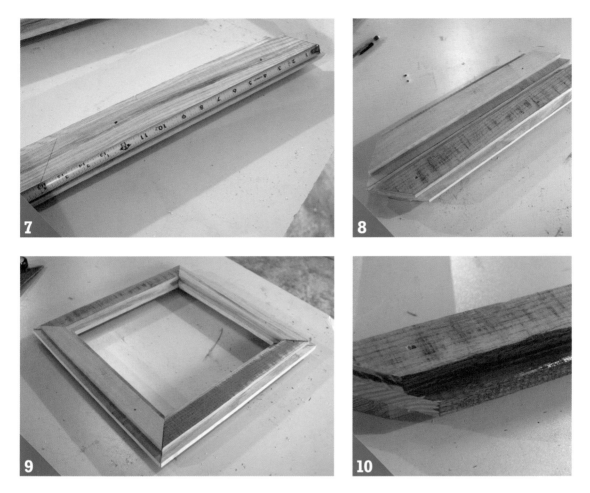

7 Measure and mark the other end of one board. I used a tape measure to mark the opposite end of one of the frame boards for the second miter cut. See the sidebar opposite to calculate the exact sizes of the framing stock.

8 Cut the marked frame board and use it to cut a second board to size. Most frames are made of two pairs of sides, and to keep everything lined up nicely, I made sure to mark the length of the second side piece in each pair directly from the first. Then, I cut the miter in the second piece. For me, this helps eliminate any potential measuring errors.

9 Check the fit. Here's a dry fit of the frame with all the joinery cut, prior to adding glue. This is the time to adjust your mitered corners as necessary before gluing.

10 Add shellac. To add some depth and drama to the finish, I applied a layer of orange shellac to the edges of the frame boards and the entire exposed surface of the middle piece (B) in each board. This was easy for me to do prior to assembly.

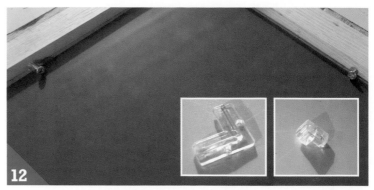

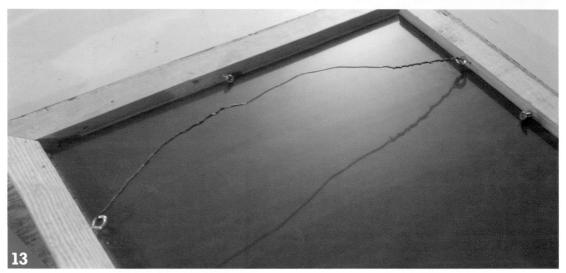

Be careful when handling unframed mirrors. Unless you specify, most glass shops leave the edges of mirrors raw, which means they're extremely sharp. For an extra dollar or two, you can ask to have the edges swiped, or buffed down to the point where the mirror can easily be handled without fear of injury. I usually get mirrors cut at my local home improvement store because I can have it done on the spot at a great price, but the store doesn't have the ability to swipe the edges. Buyer beware!

11 **Assemble the frame.** Glue and nails will provide plenty of strength for these corners.

12 **Secure the mirror.** I flipped the frame on its face and inserted the mirror from the back. At first, I used a couple of screws to temporarily hold the mirror in place. After I had the chance to run to the hardware store, I picked up a few plastic fasteners that I used to replace the screws because they looked a little nicer. The one pictured on the right is the one I ended up using.

13 **Attach a hanger.** If you're looking for a secure way to mount your mirror, consider using picture frame wire. It attaches to two small eye screws in the frame boards and is quite sturdy.

Basic Box

Have It, Hold It, Keep It Real

So many elements of woodworking can be traced back to the simple task of building boxes. Even a high-end kitchen cabinet is basically just a large box with a fancy door on it. That doesn't mean it's *easy* to build fine cabinetry right off the bat, of course, but because box making is such a fundamental skill in woodworking, I thought I would cover it here. The following steps will give you the basic skills and some practice at box making that you can then transfer to other projects. Plus, by the end you'll have a nice finished box you can use or give away as a gift.

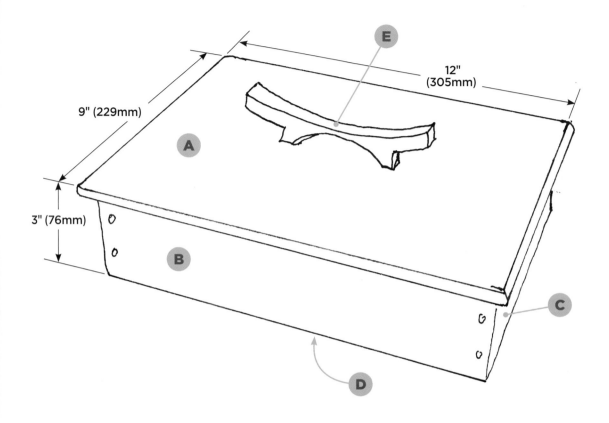

Basic Box Materials List[*]

	item	quantity	materials	dimensions
A	Lid	1	½" (13mm)-thick stock	9" x 12" (229 x 305mm)
B	Long sides	2	¾" (19mm)-thick stock	2½" x 11" (64 x 279mm)
C	Short sides	2	¾" (19mm)-thick stock	2½" x 6½" (64 x 165mm)
D	Bottom	1	¼" (6mm)-thick plywood	8" x 11" (203 x 279mm)
E	Handle blank	1	⅝" (16mm)-thick stock	1½" x 6" (38 x 152mm)

*Overall project dimensions are approximate

 Fact The U.S. has more trees now than it did less than a century ago.

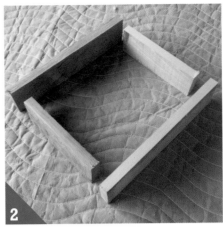

1 **Gather the materials.** Box making usually begins by laying out the stock you plan to use. Note that these four pieces have been ripped to width on the table saw and are all approximately the same thickness.

2 **Cut the side pieces to size (B and C).** In this photo, you can see that I have trimmed the side pieces (B and C) to length, and I've arranged them the way I plan to assemble them. This picture illustrates a common question you'll encounter with woodworking projects: What part overlaps another part? In this case, the answer is that the long side pieces (B) overlap the ends of the short side pieces (C) and capture the short side pieces between them. This distinction is sometimes crucial to having things line up and fit properly.

3 **Sand the side boards (B and C).** Because I wanted a little bit of character to show through, I used my belt sander to smooth the parts of the side boards (B and C) that would be exposed in the final project. The amount of cleanup you do through rough milling is a matter of personal taste.

4 **Glue the sides together (B and C).** When the side boards (B and C) were ready, I put them together using glue at the joints. Then, I clamped the whole assembly while the glue dried so the joints closed up neatly.

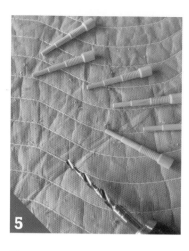

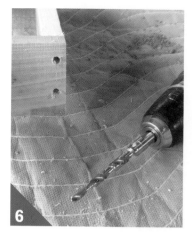

5 Consider extra security. You can leave your box as it is, secure the joints with nails, or secure the joints with Miller dowels like the ones pictured. Using Miller dowels is a simple system for securing the joints of a box. It is also easy, inexpensive, and effective; Miller dowels really should be issued to all woodworkers at birth. To use Miller dowels, select two dowels for each joint and a tapered drill bit of the same size.

6 Drill holes for the dowels. I marked and drilled two tapered holes into my box at each joint. I then filled the holes with glue.

7 Insert the dowels. Using a mallet, I drove a Miller dowel into each hole as far as it would go. Later, I cut the dowels flush with the box using a handsaw.

8 Attach the bottom (D). Every box needs a bottom, and the simplest way to add one is by screwing or nailing a ¼" (6mm)-thick piece of plywood, cut to size, to the bottom edges of the box's side boards. I used glue and my brad nail gun to attach the bottom (D) quickly and easily. You can also glue the bottom in place, or attach it with glue and then secure it with nails, screws, or brads.

9 Flush cut the dowels. Use a handsaw to cut away the portions of the Miller dowels that stick out from the box. Then, give the corners a light sanding. Here's how a corner of my box looked after this step. You can see the box has a deliberate mix of rough and smooth surfaces.

10

11

12

13

10 **Cut the lid to size (A).** Not every box needs a lid, but I wanted mine to have one, so I glued up three boards to create a wide enough blank (A). You can make your lid by cutting a piece of stock to size or gluing smaller pieces together as I did.

11 **Attach the inner lid board.** Once the glue was dry on my lid, I glued a smaller board to its underside to lock the lid in place and keep it from wiggling around when I put it on my box. Make sure this inner lid piece will fit inside your box before gluing it in place.

12 **Round the edges.** I rounded the top edges of my box lid (A) to create the refined look I was after. The easiest way to do this is with a handheld router with a round over bit.

13 **Make and attach a handle (E).** Crafting unique handles is one of my favorite box-making steps. I used to sell jewelry boxes to art galleries in batches of twenty-five or more, and I never made the same handle twice. It is a great way to show off your creativity. In this case, I made the handle (E) and stained it black. Then, I used sandpaper to distress the edges and let some of the lighter wood color shine through. I used super glue to attach the handle to the box lid. If you're just starting out, you can make a very basic handle by gluing a piece of stock to the top of your lid that is tall enough to allow you to grip it and lift the lid away from the box.

Magazine Display Box

Show Your Rustic Stuff

I reside in Salt Lake City, Utah, a city large enough to have a lot of interesting local publications. One of my favorites is *Edible Wasatch* magazine, which celebrates local food and food culture. I have been a reader since the magazine's inception two years ago, and the owners recently approached me through my custom woodworking business to see if I would build some custom display boxes for use at local retail outlets where the magazine is sold. One requirement they had was that the materials used to build the displays should be 100 percent reclaimed. That was an easy request to fulfill, as I was hip-deep in pallet wood at the time. The overall dimensions of the display boxes were largely dictated by the size of the magazines. The magazine owners also liked the concept of mimicking the style of old fruit crates with the displays. After talking it over and building a couple of prototypes for *Edible Wasatch*, I decided to photograph the construction process as part of this book to illustrate how versatile pallet wood is and how it can be used for more than just residential projects. You can use this box to display your favorite publications, or use it for any other display or storage purpose you like.

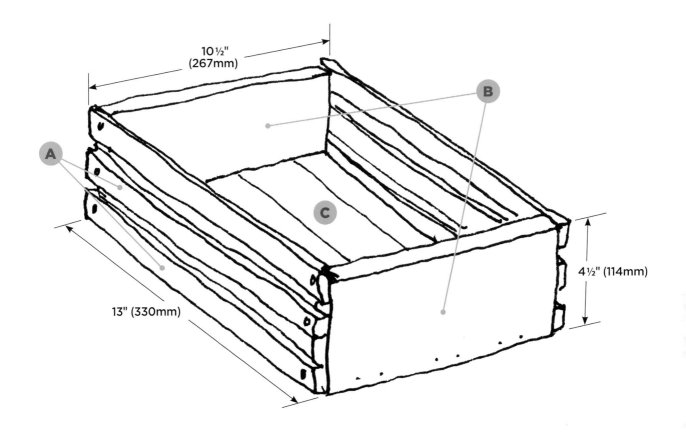

Magazine Display Box Materials*

	item	quantity	materials	dimensions
A	Side slats	6	¼" (6mm)-thick stock	1⅛" x 13" (29 x 330mm)
B	Front and back panels	2	¾" (19mm)-thick stock	4½" x 10" (114 x 254mm)
C	Bottom slats	3	½" (13mm)-thick stock	2½" x 11½" (64 x 292mm)

*Overall project dimensions are approximate

 Less than 3 percent of pallets find their way to landfills, but if they do, they're almost entirely biodegradable.

1 **Cut the front and back panels to size (B).** Each display box has a front and back panel (B), and because these are the largest components of the box, I started by cutting them to size. Of course, I was making forty-five boxes, so my stack of panels is probably more than you need (unless you want forty-five magazine display boxes of your own!).

2 **Cut the side slats to the proper width and thickness (A).** Each box requires six side slats (A). I used my table saw to rip the slats to the required width and thickness. Again, I needed more than two hundred slats for the forty-five boxes I was making. You shouldn't need nearly as many.

3 **Cut the side slats to length (A).** To cut the slats (A) to length, I used my chop saw, cutting several at once to save time and ensure uniformity.

4 **Sand the side slats (A).** Each side slat (A) needed to be sanded on the stationary belt sander to prevent splinters and create an interesting visual texture.

5 **Attach the slats (A) to the panels (B).** To attach the slats (A) to the panels (B), I began by gluing and nailing the bottom end of three slats to one edge of the front panel. Once dry, I nailed the top end of the slats to one edge of the back panel. Then I flipped the box over and repeated the process to secure the remaining slats to the other edge of the front and back panels.

6 **Attach the bottom slats (C).** The bottom of each box consists of a row of three slats (C), affixed to the box with brad nails.

7 **Celebrate a job well done.** Here's the job for *Edible Wasatch* partway done—and here's to the power of old pallets!

Furniture,
INDOORS AND OUT

Furniture can be expensive. Even shopping conservatively, if you're looking to furnish an entire room, the price can add up quickly. To avoid extreme furniture sticker shock, try making some of the pieces you need from pallet wood. Take a look at some of the furniture projects in this chapter and the gallery. If you're not quite convinced that pallet wood is the best furniture solution for you, consider the following:

- Pallet wood costs almost nothing
- A single pallet might have enough wood for multiple pieces of furniture
- Pallet wood can be cleaned up or left with its original rugged appearance, meaning it can be adapted to fit your personal style and room décor
- Pallet furniture can be used indoors or outside
- Building your own furniture gives you the opportunity to make one-of-a-kind pieces that can't be purchased anywhere else
- Building your own furniture eliminates the need to spend your time and gas money travelling from store to store shopping and looking for sales

Have I convinced you yet? If you're still feeling unsure, start small. Make an end table or another inconspicuous piece of furniture and see how you like it. I guarantee you'll want to make more.

Chair, page 71.

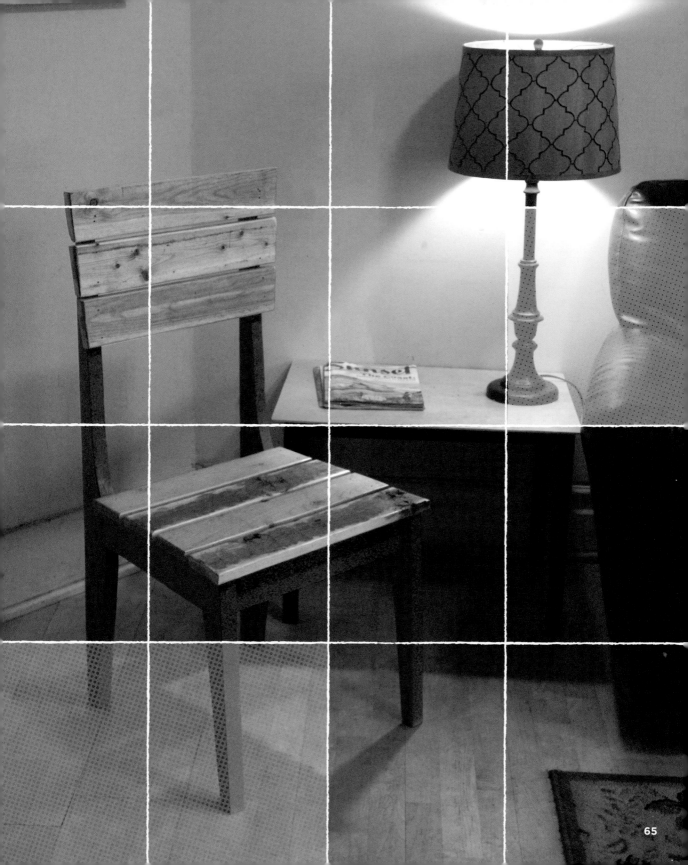

Entry Caddy

Friendly and Reliable

Ever misplace your keys? Need a place to hang a scarf, or maybe the dog's leash, right by the door so it's easy to grab on your way out? That's exactly the inspiration behind this entry caddy. You can build it however you like; I figured combining a large mirror with some useful hooks and a small shelf would add a lot of functionality to an entryway. I also painted the whole thing a really zippy blue because I just happened to like the color. Paint or stain your entry caddy any way you like.

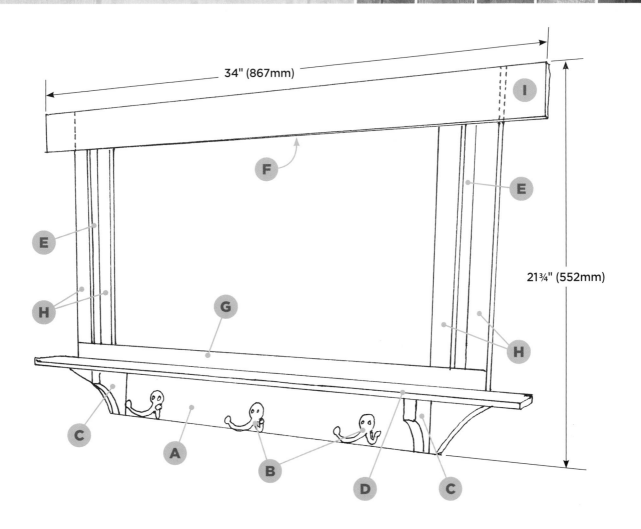

34" (867mm)

21¾" (552mm)

Entry Caddy Materials List*

	item	quantity	materials	dimensions
A	Hook strip	1	1" (25mm)-thick stock	4" x 30" (102 x 762mm)
B	Coat hooks	3		
C	Brackets	2	1" (25mm)-thick stock	3½" x 4" (89 x 102mm)
D	Shelf	1	¾" (19mm)-thick stock	4½" x 34" (114 x 867mm)
E	Mirror frame sides	2	½" (13mm)-thick stock	2½" x 17" (64 x 432mm)
F	Mirror frame top rail	1	½" (13mm)-thick stock	2½" x 30" (64 x 762mm)
G	Mirror frame bottom rail	1	½" (13mm)-thick stock	1" x 30" (25 x 762mm)
H	Mirror frame filler strips	4	½" (13mm)-thick stock	1⅛" x 13½" (29 x 343mm)
I	Mirror cap rail	1	½" (13mm)-thick stock	2½" x 34" (64 x 867mm)

*Overall project dimensions are approximate

1 Design your caddy. Designing the entry caddy couldn't be simpler. I started by laying out a row of coat hooks (B) on the board I planned to use for the hook strip (A). I didn't worry about attaching them at this stage; I just wanted to think about how many I might use, and how they might be spaced out. I also used a French curve to mark an eye-pleasing curve at one end of the hook strip board (A).

2 Cut the curve for the hook strip and mark the second. After cutting out the curve in the one end of the hook strip board (A), I used the cutout piece as a template to mark and cut the other side. This way, I knew both curves would be the same.

3 Cut the brackets to size (C). I used my band saw to cut out a pair of brackets (C) that I planned to use to hold up the shelf (D) that would run over top of the row of hooks.

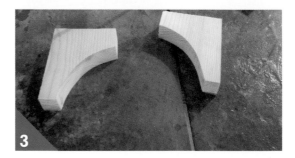

Fact Wood is the primary source of energy for things like cooking and warmth for about 50 percent of the world's population.

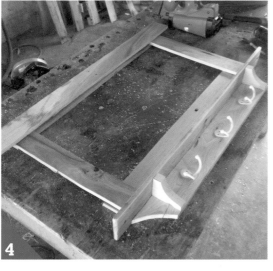

4 Attach the brackets (C). I screwed the brackets (C) into the hook strip (A), and then began to cut some of the other pieces of wood and lay them out to get a sense of how they might fit together.

5 Build the mirror frame. To keep things simple, I decided to build the mirror frame by placing the top and bottom rails (F and G) over the side pieces (E) and attaching them at their corners with countersunk screws. I then attached the cap rail (I) to the top rail (F) and the filler strips (H) to the side pieces (E). The inset image is a shot of one of the upper corners, turned upside down. You can see the cap rail, top rail, one side piece, and the edge of one of the filler strips.

6 **Build the lower shelf piece.** I attached the shelf (D) to the top of the brackets (C) in the hook strip (A). Then, I attached the mirror frame to the lower shelf piece by running screws up through the shelf (D) into the bottom edge of the bottom rail (G).

7 **Finish as desired.** Painting this project was fast and fun. The rough-sawn lumber didn't take the paint perfectly evenly, which played right into my hands, as I wanted a finish that had a shabby-chic look to it. I even used some 80-grit sandpaper to sand the paint off some of the edges to add to the distressed look of the frame.

8 **Attach the hooks (B).** Before I screwed the coat hooks (B) in, I spray-painted them in an antique bronze finish. I preferred this to the white color they were originally.

9 **Secure the mirror.** I used small plastic clips to securely attach the mirror.

Chair

Simple Meets Sophisticated

Most people who see this chair immediately recognize that the slats on the back and seat come from a pallet, but they assume I used "nicer" wood for the frame. Ha! This is just the response I had hoped for. I painted the frame blue, partly because I liked the look, but also because I wanted to emphasize the character of the seat and back slats, and the blue paint helped the frame to visually fade into the background, so to speak.

The reality, of course, is that all of the wood used in this chair came from a single pallet, and when I tell people that, it usually takes a minute to sink in. Am I trying to play mind games with people? Absolutely not. I'm just showing that while pallet wood can be used in ways that celebrate its rough and rustic nature, it can also be cleaned up and used as conventional lumber often is. (The actual construction techniques are basically the same used in fine furniture construction, so there is a nice tutorial to be had here for those interested in the logistics of chair making.)

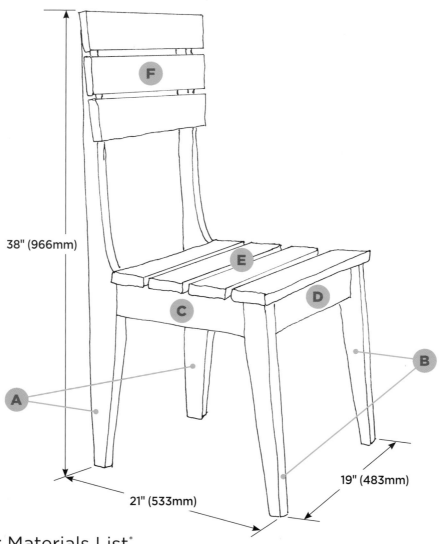

38" (966mm)

21" (533mm)

19" (483mm)

Chair Materials List*

	item	quantity	materials	dimensions
A	Rear legs	2	1" (25mm)-thick stock	4" x 38" (102 x 966mm)
B	Front legs	2	1" (25mm)-thick stock	4" x 17⅜" (102 x 442mm)
C	Side stretchers	2	1" (25mm)-thick stock	4" x 13" (102 x 330mm)
D	Front and rear stretchers	2	1" (25mm)-thick stock	4" x 17" (102 x 432mm)
E	Seat slats	4	⅝" (16mm)-thick stock	3" x 19" (76 x 483mm)
F	Back slats	3	⅝" (16mm)-thick stock	3" x 19" (76 x 483mm)

*Overall project dimensions are approximate

1 Find a suitable pallet and disassemble it. This was a good pallet; I was able to build the entire chair from it and have some slats left over. I kept the center slats as wide as possible because I knew I'd need them later for the back and seat.

2 Cut the boards to length and set aside any extras. Here are the center slats that I got from this pallet. It turned out to be way more than I needed, frankly, and some of them were nice and wide. I set them aside for other projects, because wide boards are always coveted around the shop.

3 See how the frame pieces fit together. During my fifteen-year career as a full-time furniture-maker, I've built dozens of chairs, and the process usually begins with laying out some of the parts to see how they'll relate to each other. Start with a rear leg (A), front leg (B), and side and front stretchers (C and D). The seat needs to be about 18" (457mm) from the floor, and 16" (406mm) of depth is common, but the rest is up to you. Mark just one of each of the frame pieces; you will cut them in step 6 and then use the cut pieces as patterns in step 7.

4 Determine the angle of the front leg (B). I wanted the front leg (B) to flare out a bit, and I decided to accomplish this by trimming the front end of the side stretcher (C) at an angle. I used an angle finder to determine the precise angle and mark it on the side stretcher. In my case, the angle was 5 degrees.

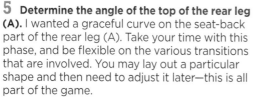

5 **Determine the angle of the top of the rear leg (A).** I wanted a graceful curve on the seat-back part of the rear leg (A). Take your time with this phase, and be flexible on the various transitions that are involved. You may lay out a particular shape and then need to adjust it later—this is all part of the game.

6 **Determine the taper of the legs, and then cut all pieces as marked.** I chose to taper the lower parts of the front and rear legs (A and B), which created a more refined look.

7 **Use the cut pieces as patterns to mark the other half of the frame pieces, then cut.** Once I had the tapers established on the legs (A and B), I used them as patterns for the other half of the chair, thus ensuring that the sides of the chair would be mirror images. Repeat the process on the other frame pieces.

8 **Drill holes for dowels to join the front legs, side stretchers, and rear legs (A, B, and C).** I decided to join the parts using dowels because they make strong joints that don't show. A drilling jig like this will set you back around $35, and it is essential equipment. It can help you drill centered holes on just about all stock that is less than 2" thick.

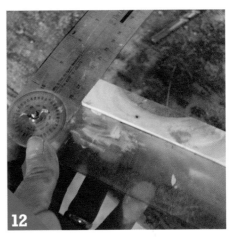

9 **Test the fit of the joints.** This photo shows how a dowel joint goes together. You'll want to test the fit of each joint to make sure the holes you drilled fit the dowels properly before you glue everything in place.

10 **Glue the chair sides together and clamp to dry.** Glue one back leg (A) and one front leg (B) to each end of a side stretcher (C).

11 **Check the sides for accuracy and adjust as needed.** Chairs need two identical sides. I double-check my chair sides by placing them on top of each other and looking for inconsistencies.

12 **Angle the ends of the front stretcher (D).** The ends of the front stretcher (D) need to be cut at 5-degree angles so the chair's width will taper from front to back.

 Fact Due to sustainable logging practices, the number of new trees each year exceeds the number of harvested trees.

13 **Glue and clamp the front stretcher (D) in place.**
Glue the sides of the chair to the front stretcher (D) and clamp them in place to dry. With the stretcher glued and clamped into place, the whole thing starts to really look like a chair.

14 **Secure the front stretcher (D) with screws and cover the ends with wooden pegs.** To really lock the front stretcher (D) into place, I ran 3" (76mm)-long screws into it. First, I predrilled ³⁄₃₂" (2.5mm)-diameter holes for the screws through the tops of the front legs (B) into the front stretcher (D) so that I didn't split the wood. Then, I counterbored small recesses to hide the screw heads. Once the screws were in, I covered their heads with small wooden plugs that I cut flush to the sides of the front legs of the chair.

15 **Cut and attach the rear stretcher (D).** I installed a rear stretcher (D) in the same way I installed the front stretcher, which completed the big structural work on the chair. This included cutting the ends of the rear stretcher at a 5-degree angle like I did with the front stretcher. After a light sanding, it was ready for paint, and then for the slats to be attached.

16 **Finish or paint the chair frame and the seat and back slats (E and F), and then attach the slats.**
To simplify the finishing process, I painted the frame of the chair prior to attaching the slats. I used spray paint, because I had some on hand, and used two coats. Once the paint was dry (which took less than fifteen minutes in my dry climate), I then applied an even coat of polyurethane to the seat and back slats (E and F). Then, I attached the slats to the chair using two-part epoxy and 1½" (38mm) brad nails.

Coffee Table

Robust and Refined

As a furniture-maker by trade, I made a choice long ago to work on a custom basis, which means I am open to working in a number of different styles. This has the advantage of providing me with a larger pool of potential customers, because I can meet a variety of challenges, but it has the minor downfall of distracting me from my passions more than I might like. In terms of woodworking, I am nuts about furniture in the Danish Modern tradition, and I always wish I had more time to devote to projects in that style. Luckily for me, the planets aligned during the writing of this book. I wanted to build a piece of furniture that was fairly refined in order to show just how versatile pallet wood can be, and my wife and I had wanted a new coffee table for our living room. Oh, happy day!

For you curious readers out there, Danish Modern is a sort of umbrella term used to describe furniture that was built in or near Denmark from about 1950–1970. There is plenty of American-made stuff that fits into this category, too, if you're not sweating the details. Generally, furniture of this style is sturdy without looking overly chunky; the overall appearance usually combines sleek lines and soft curves, which creates a rather refined aesthetic. Typical material choices include teak, walnut, and mahogany. Many furniture companies produced pieces in this style, and dining sets, hutches, and chairs are some of the most common surviving examples of the tradition.

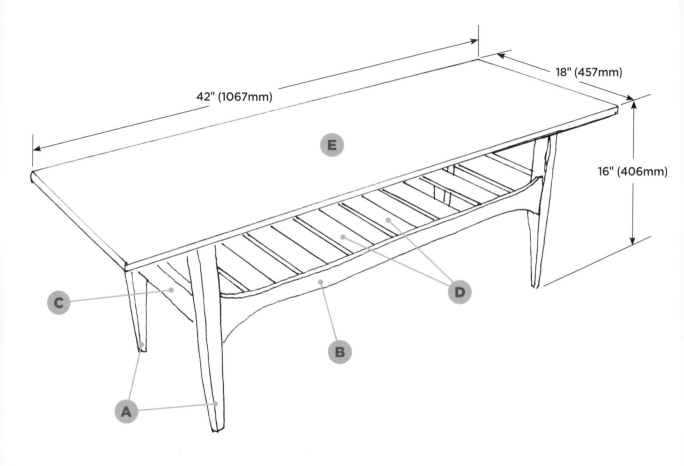

42" (1067mm)

18" (457mm)

16" (406mm)

E

C

D

B

A

Coffee Table Materials List*

	item	quantity	materials	dimensions
A	Legs	4	2" (51mm)-thick stock	2" x 15¼" (51 x 378mm)
B	Long stretchers	2	⅞" (22mm)-thick stock	4" x 29" (102 x 737mm)
C	Short stretchers	2	⅞" (22mm)-thick stock	4" x 11" (102 x 279mm)
D	Slats	7	¾" (19mm)-thick stock	2" x 12½" (51 x 318mm)
E	Top	1	¾" (17mm)-thick plywood	18" x 42" (457 x 1067mm)

*Overall project dimensions are approximate

Fact   The wood used to build pallets isn't considered "pretty" and would likely be discarded if it weren't turned into a pallet.

1 **Select the wood for the legs and begin planning the base.** I began the base by picking out some matching chunks of wood that could become the legs (A). This jumbled pile didn't look like much at the start, but I saw these pieces had the potential to be milled into something awfully nice.

2 **Clean up any wood pieces you select.** To proceed, I had to free the leg blanks (A) of any ancillary scraps of lumber and make sure all the nails were removed. When possible, I like to simply discard nail-filled pieces of pallet wood, but here I had no choice; these leg blanks were the best I had to work with, so I took the time to manually remove the nails.

3 **Trim the legs (A) to size and begin laying out the design.** With the nails removed, I could run the leg blanks over my table saw to trim them down to more refined size of 1¾" x 1¾" x 15¼" (44 x 44 x 387mm) leg blanks (A). This allowed me to start laying out some of the other parts of the table to see how they would relate to each other. Note that I used plywood instead of pallet wood for the top panel (E). It was a scrap piece of plywood, though, so it was still a recycled component. You can choose to use pallet wood for the top if you desire, or select a piece of plywood or hardwood. The design is entirely up to you.

4 **Create a groove in the long stretchers (B) and shape them.** Now that I had my leg blanks (A), I moved on to the long stretchers (B). You can see the stock I selected had a groove running down the center. I used this groove to hold the slats (D) for the table. Your long stretchers don't need this groove; you can attach the slats to the top of the long stretchers. If you're looking to replicate what I did, though, select stock with a premade groove or create the groove yourself. You can cut the groove on the table saw or glue two slats to one side of each long stretcher, leaving space between the slats for the groove. For my coffee table, I marked the spot where the long horizontal stretcher (B) would meet the legs (A), and I drew in the curves on the stretcher where I planned to cut away some excess material. Then, I used my band saw to remove the extra stock. I placed the long stretcher I had already cut on the blank for the second and used it to make an identical second long stretcher (B).

5 **Mark the taper of the legs (A).** The legs of Danish Modern furniture pieces often have some kind of curve or taper flair. Sometimes, this is accomplished by turning the legs on a lathe. While I have a lathe, and considered using it for this project, I had a hunch that a similar result could be achieved without it. So, I decided to draw a simple taper on the lower portion of the legs (A).

6 Build a tapering jig or prepare a store-bought jig. To cut the tapers, I built a simple tapering jig for my table saw. While you can buy adjustable versions of this jig for about $20 at many retail outlets, I've never gotten around to spending the money on one. In just a few minutes, and using only scrap materials, you can build one that matches your project's specs exactly. Make a base using ½" to ¾" (13 to 19mm)-thick plywood. The only requirement for the base is that it be slightly longer than your workpiece. Then, determine the angle of the taper you want to cut on your workpiece. I do this by simply drawing a line on the workpiece, which shows the excess to be trimmed away. Once you've marked the line for the taper, place your workpiece on the jig's plywood base and align the long edge of the base with the mark you drew on your workpiece; I usually just eyeball this. Once you've positioned the workpiece on the base, screw a couple of scraps to the base along the edges of the workpiece to hold it in place. The final touch is to add a toggle clamp to lock the workpiece down and keep it from shifting while you run the whole jig along the fence of your table saw. The best thing about using a tapering jig is that once you set it to your specifications, you can use it to cut the same taper over and over again without having to measure and mark the taper on each piece of wood.

7 Cut the taper on the legs (A). Here's the tapering jig in action. The leg blank (A) is held in place while the blade cuts off the waste material in one smooth cut. I decided to taper each leg on two adjacent faces, which helped create the refined look that this coffee table needed.

8 Check your progress. It is a good idea, after each step, to lay out the pieces for the coffee table to make sure everything has been cut as you desired and will fit together the way you want. That way, you can make adjustments immediately instead of realizing you need to make changes after you've done all the work and are ready to assemble the table.

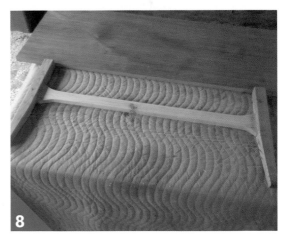

9 Round the edges of all the pieces. To keep the table feeling light and refined instead of overly chunky, I used a small hand-held trim router to round over the edges of all the parts (A, B, C, D, and E). This made a huge difference.

10 Attach the long stretchers (B) to the legs (A). I joined the long stretchers (B) to the legs (A) by gluing the parts together and then countersinking two 3" (76mm)-long screws at each joint. With the long sides assembled, my table was really beginning to take shape.

Fact Trees grow from the top, not the bottom. A branch's location on a tree will only move up the trunk a few hundred inches in 1,000 years.

11 Attach one short stretcher (C). To join the long sides, I installed a pair of short stretchers (C). They were so short that I didn't try to add curves or flares—I just kept them simple. For now, only attach one short stretcher. You'll need to insert the slats (D) before you add the second short stretcher.

12 Insert the slats (D) and then attach the second short stretcher (C). Remember those grooves in the long stretchers discussed during Step 4? Here's where I revisited them. Prior to putting in the final short stretcher, I installed a series of slats (D) in the grooves of the long stretchers (B) and nailed them into place. The resulting slatted shelf is a classic Danish Modern design element. Remember, if your long stretchers don't have a grove, you can create one, or attach your slats to the tops of the stretchers. Once you've added the slats (D), attach the second short stretcher (C).

13 **Add a stain, finish, or paint as desired to all the parts.** I was going for a kind of vintage look with this piece—I wanted people who saw it to assume it was an old thrift store find. To accomplish this, I mixed a couple of stains together and applied them deliberately to the table with the result I was looking for in mind. It was easy, and it worked. In the end, I used two coats of stain in slightly different colors, and I made my application a bit patchy to create the illusion that wear had occurred over a number of years and then been inexpertly repaired. Both coats of stain were oil-based varnishes; the first was a rich brown (Minwax Dark Walnut), while the second (Minwax Red Mahogany) had a bit more red in it. The combination of these stains created a nuanced, layered look that was more interesting than simply using a single coat or even two coats of the same product. I followed up the staining process with two coats of clear polyurethane.

14 **Attach the top (E).** I attached the top (E) by epoxying it to the tops of the legs, and then inserting small brad nails to temporarily hold it in place.

Outdoor Loveseat

Life of the Lawn Party

When the weather is nice, my family and I do a lot of entertaining outdoors, which means there is a premium on seating. No matter how many chairs and benches we have, we occasionally host a get-together where we run short of chairs. This year, we decided to add a funky loveseat to our motley outdoor seating collection. The fact that it is made from an old pallet will probably make it among the most popular seats outside the house.

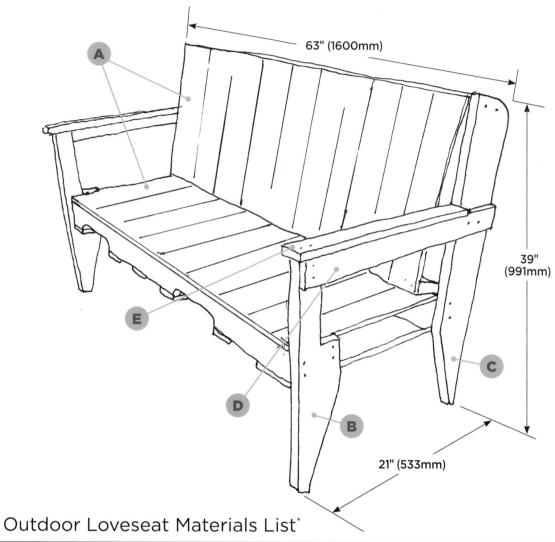

63" (1600mm)

39" (991mm)

21" (533mm)

Outdoor Loveseat Materials List*

	item	quantity	materials	dimensions
A	Seat/back pallets	2	5" (127mm)-thick pallet	21" x 60" (533 x 1524mm)
B	Front legs	2	1½" (38mm)-thick stock	5½" x 27" (140 x 686mm)
C	Rear legs	2	1½" (38mm)-thick stock	5½" x 39" (140 x 991mm)
D	Side stretchers	2	1" (25mm)-thick stock	3" x 21" (76 x 533mm)
E	Arms	2	1" (25mm)-thick stock	4" x 17" (102 x 432mm)

*Overall project dimensions are approximate

 Fact   Pallets are manufactured from a variety of materials, but wood pallets are the most popular because they are durable, green, and inexpensive.

1 **Select the seat/back pallet (A).** While most of the projects in this book are made from individual pieces of lumber harvested from pallets, this loveseat takes advantage of a fully assembled pallet. I noticed that this particular pallet was unique in the way that it was built; instead of having one center 2x4, it had two. I was able to use this to my advantage to create this project.

2 **Trim away any damage.** Because my pallet (A) had sustained some damage on one end, I decided to trim away that portion.

3 **Cut the pallet in half lengthwise (A).** The unusual construction of this pallet—I haven't seen another one like it—made me realize I could use a reciprocating saw to cut the pallet (A) lengthwise into two mirrored halves.

>>> **THE PERFECT LOVESEAT PALLET**

The pallet I used to construct this project was a great find, and you might not be able to locate one just like it right away. Don't worry, though, you can still build this pallet loveseat! Instead of using a 21" x 60" (533 x 1524mm) pallet, look for a pair of 42" x 42" (1067 x 1067mm) pallets. Cut the pallets in half to make the seat and back portions (giving you two pairs of mirrored halves instead of one as described in Step 3 of the instructions above). Bolt two of the pallet sections together to create the seat and the remaining two sections together to create the back, which will result in an 84" (2134mm)-long loveseat. If you want something a little smaller, just trim the ends of the pallets to achieve the desired dimensions. To provide support below the joint on the seat, add a center leg.

4 Begin designing the loveseat. With the pallet cut in two, it became clear that I would be able to use each half as an intact unit: one for the seat, and one for the back (A).

5 Attach the seat and back (A), then cut the front legs (B) to shape and attach. I used 3½" (89mm)-long screws to fasten the back to the seat (A). Then, I used a jigsaw to cut the front leg blanks (B) into an interesting shape. I nailed the legs into place on either side of the seat (A), attaching them to the front edge of the pallet. To temporarily hold the loveseat up so I could continue working, I inserted a scrap wood riser block under the back edge.

6 Fill the gaps in the seat (A). In an effort to keep the seat (A) as comfortable as possible, I filled in the gaps between the boards of the original pallet with wood pieces I scavenged from another pallet.

7 Cut and attach the rear legs (C) and side stretchers (D). I tapered the base of the rear leg blanks (C), and then nailed them into the thicker parts of the back and seat sections (A) to attach them. I also attached the side stretchers (D) to connect the front and rear legs (B and C) and provide a base for the arms (E). I aligned the top edge of each stretcher piece with the tops of the front legs.

8 Attach the arms (E). To create the arms (E), I installed a board on each side of the seat, attaching them to the side stretchers (D). It created a comfortable armrest as well as a good place to set a beverage.

9 Curve the tops of the rear legs (C). To soften the corner at the top of each rear leg (C), I used a jigsaw and created a curve in its place.

10 Finish the loveseat as desired. By painting the legs and arms (B, C, D, and E) of the loveseat gray, the wood tones of the seat and back really popped into prominence.

Fun & Functional
PROJECTS

All of the projects presented previously are functional (even if their function is to serve as a decoration), but the projects in this section will really go to work for you. Here, you will learn to make a toolbox and a workbench—two of the greatest workhorses in any home shop—as well as a birdhouse and a ukulele. Of course the latter two lean more toward *fun*, but they're still fully *functional*!

This section is another testament to the versatility of pallet wood. You really can use it to make just about anything you need or want, whether you desire a refined, ornamental item or one that serves a specific purpose. Pallet wood will not fail you. Keep this in mind before you start any woodworking project. Ask yourself, could I use pallets to make this? Nine times out of ten your answer will be yes, and you can cross the cost of wood from the home improvement store off your list of expenses. You are officially eco-friendly and under budget!

Birdhouse, page 92.

Birdhouse

A Homey and Hospitable Haven

I'm not much of an expert on birds—unless you want to talk about chickens, and that is a totally different topic—but I know I like my backyard a little bit more now that I've built a stylish pallet wood birdhouse and put it in just the right spot. Whether winged creatures will actually move in has yet to be determined, but because I knew I could construct this piece using free pallet wood in less than an hour, I couldn't resist the urge to give it a go. And maybe there is truth to that *Field of Dreams* saying: If you build it, they will come.

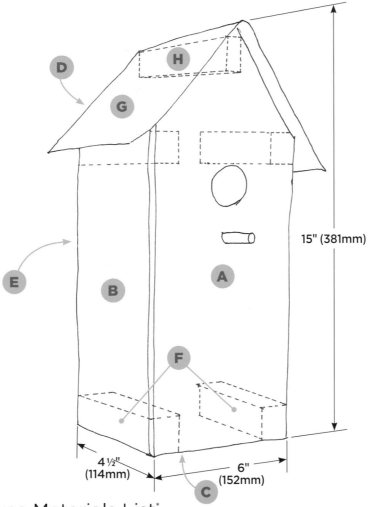

15" (381mm)

4½" (114mm)

6" (152mm)

Birdhouse Materials List*

	item	quantity	materials	dimensions
A	Front	1	½" (13mm)-thick stock	6" x 15" (152 x 381mm)
B	Sides	2	½" (13mm)-thick stock	4½" x 11" (114 x 279mm)
C	Bottom	1	½" (13mm)-thick stock	5" x 5" (127 x 127mm)
D	Gable end	1	½" (13mm)-thick stock	4" x 5" (102 x 127mm)
E	Door	1	½" (13mm)-thick stock	4¾" x 9" (121 x 229mm)
F	Corner blocks	4	⅞" (22mm)-thick stock	⅞" x 4½" (22 x 114mm)
G	Roof	1	Tin	6½" x 13" (165 x 330mm)
H	Roof beam	1	¾" (19mm)-thick stock	¾" x 4½" (19 x 114mm)

*Overall project dimensions are approximate

1 Cut the side and bottom pieces to size (B and C). When I started this project, I had a lot of pallet wood on hand, but none of the pieces were very wide. To make panels of the proper dimensions for the sides (B) and bottom (C) of the birdhouse, I glued together several narrow boards. I have a jointer in my shop, so it was quick and easy to prepare the edges of the boards, but you can just as easily use a table saw. You can use my method to create the bottom and side pieces, or cut them to size from larger stock, if it's available.

2 Cut tin for the roof to size (G). While the glue was drying on the bottom and side panels (B and C), I scrounged around and found some scrap tin to use for the roof (G). The piece I found was a leftover tile from a pressed-tin ceiling. Tin snips made it easy to cut out a piece that was just the right size.

3 Shape the roof (G). I bent the tin (G) by hand to get an approximate sense of the required size of the roof, and the angle that I might use. Note: I didn't worry about measuring the angle. A project like this does not require exacting precision and can usually be adapted as you go.

4 **Use two corner blocks (F) to begin assembling the birdhouse.** Once the glue was dry on the bottom and side panels (B and C), I removed them from the clamps, cut them to length, and began to build the birdhouse. To connect the panels, I cut out small corner blocks (F) that I placed inside the joint between the bottom and each side piece. I then used my nailer to send fasteners through the side and bottom panels and into the corner blocks.

5 **Check your progress.** The skeleton of the birdhouse is basically a U-shaped assembly. With the tin roof (G) laid out with the attached bottom and side panels (B and C), you can begin to see what the final piece will look like.

6 **Trace the birdhouse onto the front and gable blank (A and D).** I also glued up a panel for the front blank (A) and placed it on the bench below the assembly. This allowed me to trace the profile of the birdhouse—including the angled pitch of the roof—onto the panel. I also traced the profile of the birdhouse onto the gable blank (D).

Fact Keeping a wood pallet clean and usable is very easy.

7 **Cut the front piece (A) to size, attach it, and then attach the remaining corner blocks (F).** With the front panel (A) cut to size according to the tracing I made on it, I glued and screwed it to the front edge of the birdhouse assembly. I also added a pair of corner blocks along the top edges of the side pieces (B) so I would have a sturdy place where I could attach the gable piece (D).

8 **Cut and attach the gable piece (D).** The interior of a birdhouse needs to be accessible so it can be cleaned out from time to time if need be. I decided to accommodate this need by cutting the gable piece (D) to match the shape of the roof (G), but made it short enough that I would be left with a rectangular opening below it for a door after attaching it. I also nailed the roof beam (H) into the place.

9 **Cut the door (E) to size, attach it, and attach the roof (G).** I cut the stock for the door (E) to fit the rectangular opening left in the back of my birdhouse. I added notches in the bottom corners to allow it to close over the bottom corner blocks (F). The door swings on small hinges and has a latch to keep it securely closed. I also nailed the tin for the roof (G) into place.

Toolbox

Cool, Collected, Capable

While the dimensions of this toolbox may not meet your own particular needs, you can still use the simple method that follows to create a toolbox of any size by scaling the materials you use up or down to fit your needs.

The slats on many pallets usually are ½" (13mm) or less in thickness. While pieces this thin aren't ideal for every project, they're perfect as building materials for a toolbox, as it must be lightweight so that it is easily portable. A lightweight toolbox is also optimal because the tools you put inside add weight, and a toolbox too cumbersome to carry around is only moderately better than none at all. So, for this project, I recommend using pallets made of thin hardwood strips—oak and hickory are fairly common, and both offer a lot of strength, which will contribute to a durable item.

Toolboxes are not only utilitarian, they are also fun, as you can add whatever design flourishes occur to you. For example, I originally had a different idea in mind for the handle. Then, I thought of something I liked better. I think this illustrates how fun it can be to think on your feet and try different solutions to a given design challenge. Finishing methods are another way to get creative—an unfinished toolbox is perfectly acceptable, but you can always jazz things up if you're so inclined.

You may even consider building several toolboxes for different types of tools or projects. In my shed, for example, I have separate toolboxes that are organized to contain various tools that relate uniquely to plumbing, electrical, and miscellaneous carpentry tasks. Similarly, you could assign a toolbox to a router, a drill, or a jigsaw—a handy way to keep all the accessories where they're needed. A setup like this could definitely save some time around the shop.

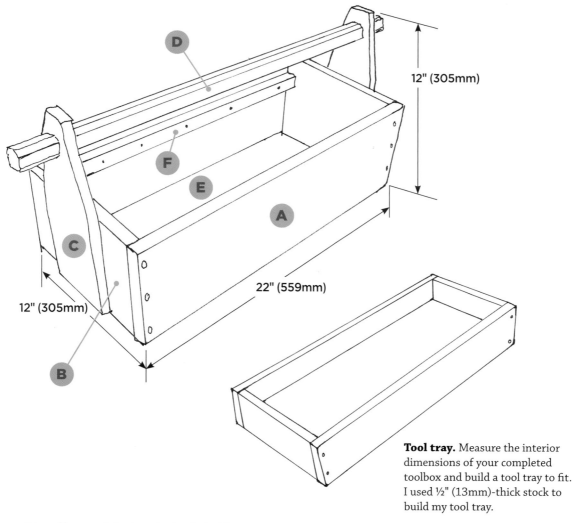

12" (305mm)

22" (559mm)

12" (305mm)

Tool tray. Measure the interior dimensions of your completed toolbox and build a tool tray to fit. I used ½" (13mm)-thick stock to build my tool tray.

Toolbox Materials List*

	item	quantity	materials	dimensions
A	Long sides	2	¾" (19mm)-thick stock	6" x 22" (152 x 559mm)
B	Short sides	2	¾" (19mm)-thick stock	6" x 10½" (152 x 267mm)
C	End caps	2	⅝" (16mm)-thick stock	5" x 12" (127 x 305mm)
D	Handle	1	1" (25mm)-thick stock	1" x 27" (25 x 686mm)
E	Bottom	1	¼" (6mm)-thick plywood	12" x 22" (305 x 559mm)
F	Sliders	2	¾" (19mm)-thick stock	1" x 20½" (25 x 521mm)

*Overall project dimensions are approximate

1 **Sand the wood as desired.** I loved the rough and rustic character of the wood I used for this project, which was fortunate, because the embedded nail heads in the wood meant I couldn't run it through my planer to quickly resurface it. I decided to use a handheld belt sander to smooth out the surface of the wood pieces and reduce the possibility of getting splinters from the finished project.

2 **Check the edges for nails, and then level.** I used my jointer to flatten and level the edges of the stock, after checking to verify there were no nails close to the edges.

3 **Square off the ends.** To square the ends of the boards and cut them to the necessary size, I used my chop saw with the angle set to 90°. Remember to check for nails before you do this.

4 **Clamp the long and short sides together for assembly (A and B).** After cutting the boards to size, I clamped the long and short sides (A and B) together to form the basic frame of the toolbox.

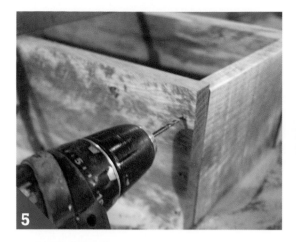

5 **Attach the long and short sides (A and B).** To join the long sides (A) to the short sides (B), I predrilled several ³⁄₃₂" (2.5)-diameter holes at each joint and then screwed in 1½" (38mm) screws.

6 **Determine the shape of the end caps (C).** Every toolbox needs a handle (D), and I planned to secure mine in place by running it through a pair of end caps (C). I decided to give the top of the end caps a tapered shape, so I marked the desired result on the end cap blanks.

7 **Cut the end caps (C) to their final size and shape.** The band saw was the perfect tool for cutting the end caps (C) down to size. You could also use a jigsaw.

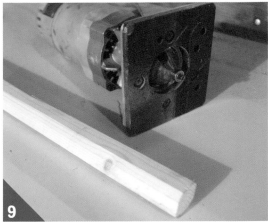

8 **Drill holes for the handle (D).** I used a 1⅛" (29mm) Forstner bit to bore a hole near the top of each end cap (C).

9 **Select a dowel for the handle (D) or shape it from stock.** Ideally, I would have used a 1⅛" (29mm)-diameter dowel for the toolbox handle (D), but because I didn't have one readily available, I ripped a piece of scrap wood into a length of 1 1⁄16" x 1 1⁄16" (27 x 27mm)-square stock. Then, I used a handheld router with a 45° chamfer bit to turn the square stock into an octagonal blank that is easy on the hands.

10 **Attach the bottom (E).** For the bottom (E), I simply glued a ¼" (6mm)-thick piece of plywood to the toolbox frame, and then screwed it in place.

11 **Attach the end caps (C) and handle (D).** I attached the end caps (C) to the sides of the toolbox with glue and screws, and then slid the handle (D) into place.

 Fewer fossil fuels are used in processing wood than processing other materials like concrete, steel, and aluminum.

12 Smooth the edges. I smoothed over the edges with a Surform plane to make sure slivers and splinters would be kept at bay.

13 Attach the sliders (F). I knew I wanted to incorporate a sliding tool tray into the toolbox design, so I mounted a set of sliders (F) just below the top edge of the box along the long sides (A).

14 Assemble the tray. The tool tray was built of ½" (13mm)-thick stock that was glued and nailed into a box. The bottom was simply glued and screwed into place. The finished tray is sturdy and easily removable so the items stored below it are accessible. The tool tray can also be removed from the toolbox to be carried around separately as needed.

Workbench

Doing a Job Well

I suppose not everybody needs or has space for a workbench, but there's no denying it is handy to have a space you can use solely for projects. And what better place to build projects than on a workbench made entirely from reclaimed pallet wood? Feel free to vary the dimensions or specifics of this project to suit your needs—the following instructions should provide you with a good starting point to create what you want.

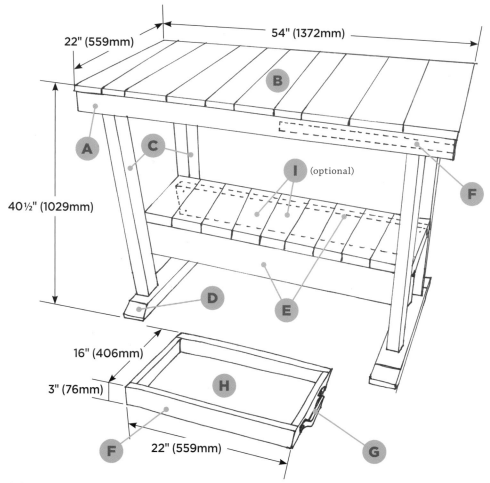

Workbench Materials List*

	item	quantity	materials	dimensions
A	Runners	2	2" (51mm)-thick stock	4" x 54" (102 x 1372mm)
B	Top slats	10 or more depending on bench size	¾" (19mm)-thick stock	22" (559mm) long, varying widths add up to 54" (1372mm)
C	Legs	4	2" (51mm)-thick stock	3" x 33¾" (76 x 857mm)
D	Feet	2	2" (51mm)-thick stock	4" x 22" (102 x 559mm)
E	Stretchers	2	2" (51mm)-thick stock	6" x 44" (152 x 1118mm)
F	Drawer sides	2	¾" (19mm)-thick stock	3" x 22" (76 x 559mm)
G	Drawer front and back	2	¾" (19mm)-thick stock	3" x 14½" (76 x 368mm)
H	Drawer bottom	1	¼" (6mm)-thick plywood	16" x 22" (406 x 559mm)
I	Bottom slats	10 or more depending on bench size	¾" (19mm)-thick stock	22" (559mm) long, varying widths add up to 54" (1372mm)

*Overall project dimensions are approximate

1 **Cut the top slats (B) to size and attach to the runners (A).** I chose to begin this project with the top. After cutting a series of slats (B) down to 22" (559mm) long, I screwed them to a pair of runners (A). This method didn't yield a perfectly flat top, but it was fine for my purposes.

2 **Attach the legs and feet (C and D).** After turning the top upside down, I fastened the legs (C) to the runners (A), and then attached the feet (D) to the bottom of each set of legs using long screws. Note: I chose to cut the ends of the feet at a pleasing angle. I built the bench upside down, as it went together more easily that way and meant that I didn't have to fuss as much about having the parts aligned along the way.

Fact Employment in the U.S. furniture industry fell more than 50 percent between 1999 and 2011.

3 Measure and attach a stretcher (E). After turning the bench on its side, I ran a thick stretcher (E) between the legs and nailed it in place using a framing nailer. I placed the bottom of the stretcher about 6½" (165mm) from the top of the foot. If you don't have a framing nailer on hand, long screws would be a good substitute to use to attach the stretcher.

4 Attach the second stretcher (E) and check your progress. With the second stretcher (E) in place, the bench could be considered complete. I decided to add a couple of finishing touches, however.

5 Attach the bottom slats (I). Adding some storage capacity to the bench is easy—just run a series of slats (I) across the tops of the stretchers (E).

6 Attach drawer slides. Because I wanted to incorporate a drawer into the design, I began by attaching a pair of drawer slides to the inside face of the runners (A) below the top slats (B) of the bench. Once both drawer slides were in, I measured the distance between them, which determined the overall width measurement for the drawer.

7 Build the drawer using the side and front and back pieces (F and G). To build the drawer, I made a simple box using ¾" (19mm)-thick stock. The lengths of the sides (F) are fairly arbitrary (I used 22" [559mm]-long pieces), and the length of the front and back pieces (G) are 1½" (38mm) less than the total width of the drawer, determined during the previous step.

8 Stain the drawer bottom (H) if desired. So the objects I kept in the drawer would stand out nicely against the drawer's bottom (H), I stained it brown prior to attaching it to the drawer box.

9 Attach the drawer bottom (H). I screwed the bottom (H) of the drawer in place. As I did so, I made sure to check that the drawer as a whole was square by comparing the diagonal measurements.

10 **Attach the drawer to the drawer slides.** Once the drawer was finished, I placed it between the drawer slides and installed it using three screws per side.

11 **Attach a drawer handle.** I had this door pull on hand to use as a handle for the drawer. It went on with just a couple of screws.

12 **Select a piece of wood to extend the workbench's surface.** As a neat bonus, the work surface of the bench can easily be extended by pulling out the drawer and capping it with a ¾" (19mm)-thick piece of plywood.

 Fact Wood pallets do not release harmful chemicals into the atmosphere.

Ukulele

Music in the Key of 'Pallet'

This cute little instrument has had a couple of moments in the limelight in American pop culture, and it is enjoying another one right now. As an acoustic music lover, and a fan of living room and front porch music, I'm all for it. If I were a reader, for me, the icing on the cake of a book about making a ukulele would be a chapter detailing how to build a ukulele using free pallet wood, so that's why I'm going for it here. I hope to show how a solid wood, fully playable instrument can be made using only pallet wood. This project is also a tip of my cap to Taylor Guitars' twenty-five limited edition pallet guitars (*www.taylorguitars.com*). Not just a novelty, the ukulele I made is definitely of nice quality. In fact, I sold the ukulele I had owned previously after I made this one, which cost me less than $20 for strings and tuners. It isn't the easiest project in this book, but it isn't rocket science, either, so if you're inclined, just take your time and you can probably make it work.

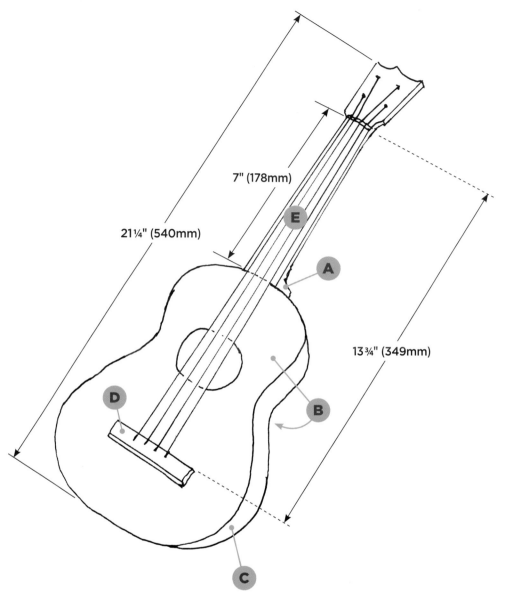

7" (178mm)

21¼" (540mm)

13¾" (349mm)

Ukulele Materials List*

	item	quantity	materials	dimensions
A	Neck blank	1	1¾" (44mm)-thick stock	2¼" x 13" (57 x 330mm)
B	Top and back	2	⅛" (3mm)-thick stock	7" x 10" (178 x 254mm)
C	Side strip**	1	⅛" (3mm)-thick stock	2¼" x 30" (57 x 763mm)
D	Bridge blank	1	⁵⁄₁₆" (8mm)-thick stock	⁵⁄₁₆" x 2½" (8 x 64mm)
E	Fingerboard blank	1	¼" (6mm)-thick stock	2" x 7" (51 x 178mm)

*Overall project dimensions are approximate
**Cut a few extra side strip pieces just in case

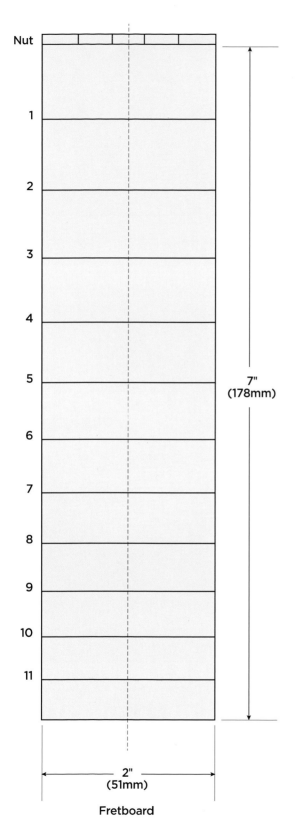

Fretboard

Fret Scale

Fret number	Distance from nut	Distance between frets
1	¾" (19mm)	Nut–Fret 1: ¾" (19mm)
2	1½" (38mm)	Fret 1–Fret 2: ¾" (19mm)
3	2³⁄₁₆" (56mm)	Fret 2–Fret 3: ⅝" (16mm)
4	2¹³⁄₁₆" (71mm)	Fret 3–Fret 4: ⅝" (16mm)
5	3⁷⁄₁₆" (87mm)	Fret 4–Fret 5: ⅝" (16mm)
6	4" (102mm)	Fret 5–Fret 6: ⁹⁄₁₆" (14mm)
7	4⁹⁄₁₆" (116mm)	Fret 6–Fret 7: ⁹⁄₁₆" (14mm)
8	5¹⁄₁₆" (129mm)	Fret 7–Fret 8: ½" (13mm)
9	5½" (140mm)	Fret 8–Fret 9: ⁷⁄₁₆" (11mm)
10	6" (152mm)	Fret 10–Fret 11: ½" (13mm)
11	6⁷⁄₁₆" (164mm)	Fret 11–Fret 12: ⁷⁄₁₆" (11mm)

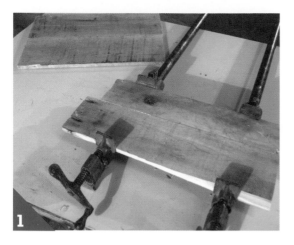

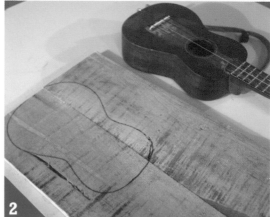

1 **Cut the top and back pieces (B) to size.** It would have been nice if I had had a wide enough board on hand to make the front and back pieces (B) of the ukulele. Because I didn't, I glued together a pair of boards to produce a wide enough blank for the front, and then I did another one for the back. If you have boards that are wide enough, simply cut them to size.

2 **Check the wood for problem areas.** Makers of fine stringed instruments usually line up any seams in the wood with the center of the instrument, but I wasn't too worried about this. I was, however, careful to avoid any flaws in the surface of the wood blanks for the front and back (B).

3 **Plane the front and back pieces (B).** Once the joint had had enough time to dry, I ran the front and back blanks (B) through my planer. The easiest way to do this was to place the blanks on a ¾" (19mm)-thick riser that I fed through the machine. I planed the blanks to about 3⁄32" (2.5mm) thick.

Fact Almost all American homes (about 90 percent!) have wood framing for their roofs and walls.

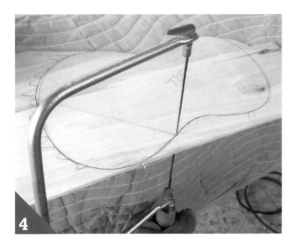

4 Draw and cut out the front and back pieces (B). Because I had a ukulele on hand, I used it as a pattern, and then cut the front and back pieces (B) out of the delicate blanks with a coping saw, as they were a bit too fragile to cut using a jigsaw or band saw. Cutting them by hand wasn't a problem in terms of time, either—it only took a few minutes to cut out each piece. If you don't have a ukulele on hand, you can find measurements online to use to size your ukulele. You can make your ukulele a variety of sizes depending on your preference for tone and sound.

5 Label the front and back pieces (B). Because I had a preference as to which side of the front and back pieces (B) I wanted to show off on the finished instrument, I made sure to label them.

6 Measure and mark the center of the sound hole. The front (B) of the ukulele needed a sound hole. I used a regular drill bit to mark the center of the hole. Use a ukulele that you have on hand or check online to determine the size and placement of the sound hole on your pallet ukulele.

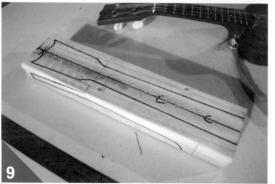

7 **Cut out the sound hole.** I drilled the sound hole in the front piece (B) with a 1¾" (44mm) hole saw. A Forstner bit would also work for this step.

8 **Draw a rough profile of the neck on the blank (A).** The next logical step was to think about the neck. I drew a rough outline for the side profile of the neck onto the side of the neck blank (A). Getting it exact isn't critical at this stage, so just try and be as close as you can. Remember: If you don't have a ukulele of your own that you can use to develop the patterns for this project, check online to find sample patterns and measurements you can use to create your pallet ukulele.

9 **Draw the design for the top of the neck on the blank (A).** By measuring a few key points on my ukulele's neck, I was able to create a drawing on the top side of the neck blank (A). Especially important are the width of the neck at the nut and bottom of the neck, and also the location of the tuning pegs. Check online for these measurements if necessary.

10 **Cut out the neck (A).** I used my band saw to cut away the waste on the neck blank (A).

11 **Sand the neck (A).** The band saw will allow you to cut quite closely to the lines drawn on the neck blank (A), but the neck will still need to be cleaned up afterword. A stationary belt sander is a good tool for this.

12 **Refine the neck details (A).** Refine any irregularities on the curved portions of the neck (A) using sanding drums in a drill press.

13 **Round the back of the neck (A).** To round over the back of the neck (A), I used a Surform plane and sandpaper.

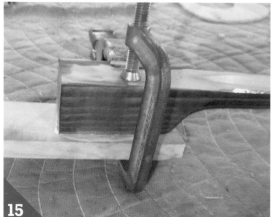

14 **Drill holes for the tuners.** Drill four holes, perpendicular to the face of the headstock in the top of the neck (A) for the tuners.

15 **Glue on additional stock to the neck as needed (A).** Partway through the project, I realized that my neck wasn't quite thick enough at the heel. To remedy this, I just glued on a block of wood at the base of the neck (A).

16 **Cut the wood added to the neck to shape (A).** Once I had cut away the excess and sanded it smooth, the addition of the heel block was barely noticeable. This is not an unusual technique for situations like the one I encountered here.

17 **Trace a mold to shape the sides (C).** To build the body of the ukulele, I bent the sides (C) from a single strip of wood, using steam. This required a mold around which to clamp the side piece. Making the mold was easy—I just traced the back piece (B) for the ukulele onto some ¾" (19mm)-thick plywood to get started.

Fact   Nebraska was the first state to observe Arbor Day in 1872; the state now boasts the largest man-planted forest in the world.

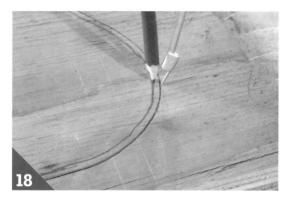

18 **Trace the mold outline.** Once I had an outline traced onto the plywood, I used a compass set to ⅛" (3mm) to trace a second outline just inside the first.

19 **Cut and attach the layers for the mold.** I cut out the plywood on the inner line, giving myself an appropriately sized piece of plywood for the mold. I traced the cutout to make two more plywood pieces of the same size, and then glued and nailed them all together to make a mold that was 2¼" (57mm) high.

20 **Steam the side strip (C) and secure it to the mold.** After steaming the strip of wood for the sides (see pages 118–119), I bent it around the mold and clamped it into place. You can see that I overlapped the ends of the side strip (C) at the top of the ukulele; I trimmed them to size later.

BENDING WOOD WITH STEAM

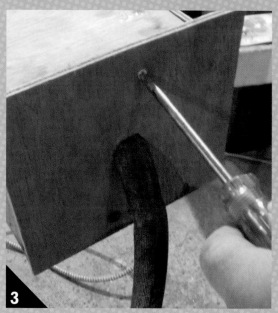

1 **Cut the side strip (C) to size and make some extras.** Steam bending is easy once you know how. You'll want to start by cutting some strips that are suited to the size of your project. In my case, I needed strips that were ⅛" (3mm) thick and 2¼" (57mm) high. I made several so I would have some extras just in case of breakage.

2 **Construct a steam chamber.** You'll need to construct a chamber of some kind—I just used scrap plywood because it was quick, easy, and free. The chamber should have a hole in each end so steam can come in one side and exit the other while your work pieces, placed in the center of the chamber, get nice and bendy.

3 **Create a removable end.** One end of your steam chamber will need to be removable so you can open it easily. It should also have an access hole for your source of steam.

4 Put a small hole in the opposite end of the chamber. A ¼" (6mm)-diameter hole in the opposite end of the chamber is all you need for the steam to escape.

5 Select a steam source and modify it as needed. The heart of my steam bender is a $30 wallpaper steamer I bought in town. My first move was to cut off the fitting on the end and insert a hose into the end cap.

6 Put your steamer to use. Use your steamer by inserting your work piece into it and turning on the steam source. When your work piece is flexible, bend it into shape around your mold and wait for it to set. In addition to making ukuleles, I also use my steam bender for banjo pots, although that's another story altogether.

21 **Trim the side piece (C), cut notches in the neck (A), and apply glue to the back (B).** After letting the clamped side piece (C) sit for a day, there was little danger of it bending out of shape, so I removed the clamps and trimmed the ends with a handsaw. I also used the same handsaw to cut small notches into the base of the neck (A) to receive the ends of the side piece (C). Finally, I prepped the back of the ukulele (B) for assembly by running a bead of glue along its edge.

22 **Glue and clamp the back, sides, and neck together (A, B, and C).** Gluing the back (B) to the side piece (C) and neck (A) looks a little chaotic, but it isn't hard. Just make sure to keep the glue from the back (B) from getting onto the mold for the sides so the mold doesn't get stuck in place!

23 **Remove the clamps and check your progress.** After a few hours, I removed the clamps and the mold.

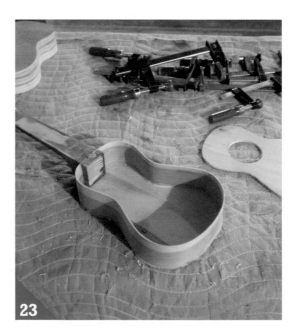

24 **Glue the top piece in place (B).** Gluing the top (B) on is pretty straightforward by comparison. Just add glue and clamp it in place.

25 **Create the fingerboard blank (E).** Once the ukulele was assembled, I turned my attention to making the fingerboard (E). This process started by holding a ¼" (6mm)-thick blank to the front side of the neck (A), and then holding the assembly upside down and using a pencil to mark the waste sections on back of the fingerboard blank (E). I then cut away the waste with my band saw a bit later.

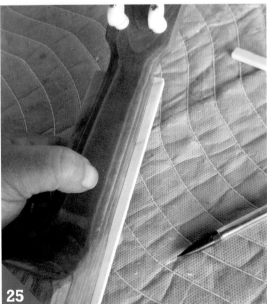

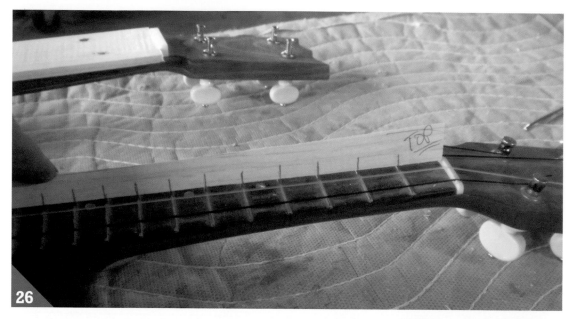

26 **Mark the locations of the frets on a story stick.** Most of the measurements for building a ukulele can be altered or you can get away with it if they're not quite exact. As long as you get an instrument of the shape and size you want, you're golden. In order for your ukulele to play properly, however, the fingerboard (E) has to be laid out correctly. To establish the correct spacing for the fret slots, I marked the locations of the frets from the ukulele I already had onto a thin piece of scrap wood called a story stick. If you're building your ukulele to the specifications on the materials list, you can use the fret measurements from the illustration for your ukulele. Otherwise, you will need to calculate the position of your frets based on the length of your ukulele's neck. There are several online fret calculators that can help you with this, like this one: *www.stewmac.com/FretCalculator*.

27 **Transfer the fret locations to the fingerboard (E).** I then took the story stick and used it to mark the fret locations on my fingerboard blank (E).

28 **Extend the lines for the fret locations.** To extend the marks for the frets into useful, straight lines, I used a square.

29 **Cut the fret slots, trim the fingerboard (E) to size, and glue in place.** After cutting the fret slots with a handsaw and miter box, I trimmed the edges of the fingerboard (E) down to size and glued it to the neck (A).

30 **Place the fretwire.** Fretwire is usually sold by the yard. I used wire clippers to snip it into 2"–3" (51–76mm) pieces that I then seated in the fret slots using a hammer. This may sound like a production, but it isn't too tough—I consider myself semi-experienced at instrument making, and I can complete a fingerboard in about fifteen minutes.

Fact   Some ancient cultures knocked on trees to summon the trees' spirits, which might be the origin of the phrase "knock on wood."

31

31 **Measure the placement of the nut and bridge (D), and glue the nut in place.** To ensure the ukulele plays in tune, the final crucial measurement is the distance between the bone nut and the top of the bridge (D) where the strings terminate. I measured this distance off my store-bought ukulele, but you can use online resources to get the measurement for yours.

32 **Make and attach the bridge (D).** I didn't have an extra piece of bone for the bridge (D), so I just made a quick and dirty bridge from—you guessed it—pallet wood. I don't regret the choice: my ukulele has plenty of volume and clarity!

32

 Fact   Almost no part of a tree goes unused when it is processed.

MAKE ME A PALLET ON THE FLOOR

Also known as *Make Me a Pallet* and *Pallet on the Floor*, *Make Me a Pallet on the Floor* is considered a classic blues song. Like many folk songs, its origins are not well known. It is believed to have originated during the 1800s, and various versions of the lyrics appeared in print in the early 1900s. W. C. Handy is often credited with the most recent version of the score. The song depicts a weary traveler who, lacking a better option, uses a wood pallet as a bed.

LYRICS

Chorus

C Make me down a pallet on your **G** floor
C Make me down a pallet on your **G** floor
Make me a **B7** pallet, **C** make it soft and low
G Make it down where my **D** good gal will never **C** know

Verse

These blues are everywhere I see
Weary blues are everywhere I see
Blues all around me, everywhere I see
Nobody's had these blues like me

Repeat Chorus

Come all you good time friends of mine
Come all you good time friends of mine
When I had a dollar you treated me just fine
Where'd you go when I only had a dime?

Repeat Chorus

Well, I'd be more than satisfied
Yes, honey, I'd be more than satisfied
When I reach Atlanta and have no place to go
Won't you make me a pallet on your floor?

Repeat Chorus

Well the way I'm sleeping, my back and shoulders're tired
The way I'm sleeping, my back and shoulders're tired
The way I'm sleeping, my back and shoulders're tired
Gonna roll right over and try it on my side

Repeat Chorus

I drink whiskey at night; eat bacon in the morning
Whiskey at night and bacon in the morning
I drink whiskey at night; eat bacon in the morning
That's about all I need to keep me going

Repeat Chorus

Been hanging around with some good friends of mine
Hanging around with some good friends of mine
Oh they treat me very nice and kind,
But where'd they go, when I haven't got a dime?

Repeat Chorus

INDEX

Note: Page numbers in italics indicate projects.

Acquisition editor: Kerri Landis   **Assistant editor:** Heather Stauffer   **Copy editor:** Paul Hambke
Cover and layout designer: Jason Deller   **Editor:** Katie Weeber   **Proofreader:** Lynda Jo Runkle
Indexer: Jay Kreider

More Great Books from Fox Chapel Publishing

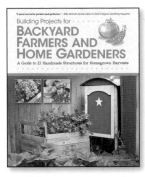

Building Projects for Backyard Farmers and Home Gardeners
ISBN 978-1-56523-543-4 **$19.95**

Art of the Chicken Coop
ISBN 978-1-56523-542-7 **$19.95**

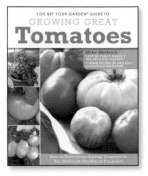

You Bet Your Garden Guide to Growing Great Tomatoes
ISBN 978-1-56523-710-0 **$14.95**

Tree Craft
ISBN 978-1-56523-455-0 **$19.95**

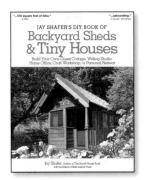

Jay Shafer's DIY Book of Backyard Sheds & Tiny Houses
ISBN 978-1-56523-816-9 **$19.99**

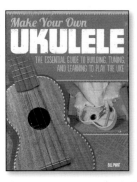

Make Your Own Ukulele
ISBN 978-1-56523-565-6 **$17.95**

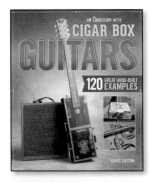

An Obsession with Cigar Box Guitars
ISBN 978-1-56523-796-4 **$14.99**

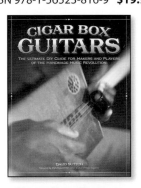

Cigar Box Guitars
ISBN 978-1-56523-547-2 **$29.95**

Handmade Music Factory
ISBN 978-1-56523-559-5 **$22.95**